Homer Greene

Coal and the Coal Mines

Homer Greene

Coal and the Coal Mines

ISBN/EAN: 9783744791694

Printed in Europe, USA, Canada, Australia, Japan

Cover: Foto ©Andreas Hilbeck / pixelio.de

More available books at **www.hansebooks.com**

COAL AND THE COAL MINES

BY

HOMER GREENE

*WITH ILLUSTRATIONS FROM DRAWINGS BY
THE AUTHOR*

BOSTON AND NEW YORK
HOUGHTON, MIFFLIN AND COMPANY
The Riverside Press, Cambridge
1889

The Riverside Press, Cambridge, U. S. A.:
Electrotyped and Printed by H. O. Houghton & Company.

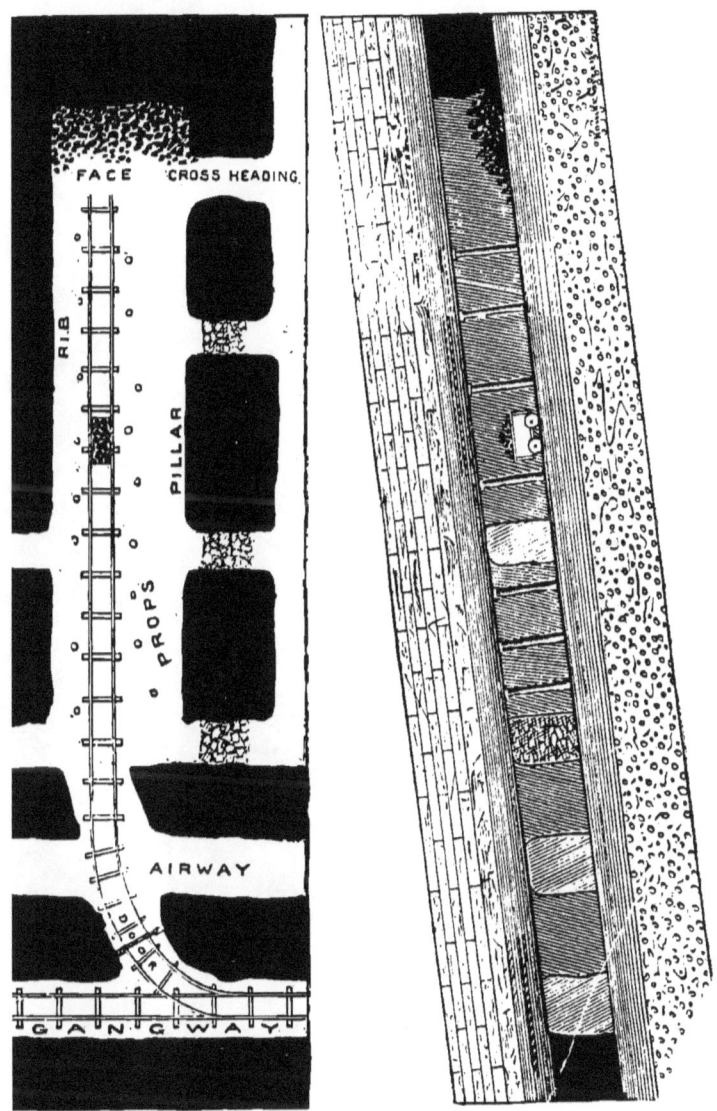

GROUND PLAN AND LONGITUDINAL SECTION OF CHA

To
MY SON,
GILES POLLARD GREENE,
WHO WAS BORN ON THE DAY THIS BOOK WAS BEGUN,
AND WHOSE SMILES AND TEARS
THROUGH HALF A YEAR
HAVE BEEN A DAILY INSPIRATION IN THE WORK,
This Completed Task
IS NOW DEDICATED
BY
THE AUTHOR.

PREFACE.

IN treating of so large a theme in so small a compass it is impossible to do more than make an outline sketch. It has been the aim of the author to give reliable information free from minute details and technicalities. That information has been, for the most part, gathered through personal experience in the mines. The literature of this special subject is very meagre, and the author is unable to acknowledge any real indebtedness to more than half a dozen volumes. First among these is the valuable treatise on "Coal Mining," by H. M. Chance of the Pennsylvania Geological Survey. Other volumes from which the author has derived considerable information are the State geological reports of Pennsylvania, the mine inspector's reports of the same State, and the "Coal Trade Annuals," issued by Frederick E. Saward of New York.

The author desires also to acknowledge his indebtedness for valuable assistance in the preparation of this work to John B. Law and Andrew Bryden, mining superintendents, and George Johnson, real estate agent, all of the Pennsylvania Coal Company, at Pittston, Pennsylvania, and to the officers of the Wyoming Historical and Geological Society of Wilkes Barre, Pennsylvania.

HOMER GREENE.

HONESDALE, Pa.,
   May 15, 1889.

CONTENTS.

CHAPTER	PAGE
I. In the Beginning	1
II. The Composition of Coal	6
III. When Coal was Formed	14
IV. How the Coal Beds Lie	22
V. The Discovery of Coal	35
VI. The Introduction of Coal into Use	51
VII. The Way into the Mines	75
VIII. A Plan of a Coal Mine	94
IX. The Miner at Work	112
X. When the Mine Roof Falls	127
XI. Air and Water in the Mines	147
XII. The Dangerous Gases	159
XIII. The Anthracite Coal Breaker	176
XIV. In the Bituminous Coal Mines	192
XV. The Boy Workers at the Mines	204
XVI. Miners and their Wages	222

COAL AND THE COAL MINES.

CHAPTER I.

IN THE BEGINNING.

EVERY one knows that mineral coal is dug out from the crust of the earth. But the question frequently is asked concerning it, How and under what conditions was it formed? In order to answer this inquiry it is necessary to have recourse to the science of geology.

A brief review of the geological history of the earth's crust will be of prime importance, and it will not be inappropriate to go back to the origin of the earth itself. But no man can begin at the beginning; that is too far back in the eternal mists; only the Infinite Mind can reach to it. There is a point, however, to which speculation can journey, and from which it has brought back brilliant theories to account for the existence of the planet on which we live. The most philosophic of these theories, as it certainly is the most popular, is the one known as the Nebular Hypothesis, propounded by Laplace, the great French astronomer, in 1796. This theory accords so well with the laws of physics, and with the human knowledge of the age, that most of the great astronomers have adopted it as the best that has been given to us, and the world of science may be said to have accepted it as final. Let us suppose, then, in accordance with this theory, that our earth was, at one time, a ball of liquid fire, revolving on its axis, and moving, in its orbit, around the parent sun with the motion imparted to it in the beginning. As cooling and condensation went on, a crust was formed on its surface, and water was formed on the crust. The waters, however, were no sooner spread out than they were tossed by the motion of the atmosphere into waves, and these waves, by constant friction against the rock crust of the earth, wore it down into pebbles, sand, and mud. The silt thus made being washed up on to the primitive rock and left there by the receding waters became again as hard and firm as before. Occasionally a subsidence, due to the contraction of the earth's body, would take place and the sea would again sweep over the entire surface, depositing another layer of silt on the one already formed, or possibly washing that again into sand and pebbles. This process continued through an indefinite period of time, forming layer upon layer of stratified rock, or excavating great hollows in the surface already formed.

That period in the history of the earth's crust

before stratification began is known as Archean time. This was followed by the period known as Paleozoic time, which is divided into three ages. The first is the age of Invertebrates. It was during this age that life made its advent on the earth. The waters were the first to bring it forth, but before the close of the age it began also to appear on the land, in isolated spots, in the simplest forms of vegetation. The next age is known as the age of Fishes, during which vegetable life became more varied and abundant, winged insects floated in the air, and great sharks and gars swam in the seas. Then came the Carboniferous age or age of Coal Plants, in which vast areas of what are now the Middle, Southern, and Western States were covered with low marshes and shallow seas, and were rich and rank with multitudinous forms of vegetation. But these marshes were again and again submerged and covered with material washed up by the waves before the final subsidence of the waters left them as a continuing portion of the dry land. It was at the close of the Carboniferous age that great disturbances took place in the earth's crust. Before this the rock strata had been comparatively level; now they were folded, flexed, broken, rounded into hills pushed resistlessly up into mountain ranges. It was at this time that the upheaval of the great Appalachian Range in North America took place. Following this came Mesozoic time, which had but one age, the age of Reptiles. It was during this age that the type of reptiles reached its culmination. The land generally brought forth vegetation, though not with the prolific richness and luxury of the Carboniferous age. Birds, insects, and creeping things were abundant, and monsters of the saurian tribe swam in the seas, roamed through the marshes, crawled on the sandy shores, and took short flights through the air. The last great division is known as Cenozoic time, and covers two ages, the age of Mammals and the age of Man. It was during the mammalian age that trees of modern types, such as oak, maple, beech, etc., first made their appearance, and mammalian animals of great variety and size, both herbivorous and carnivorous, roamed through the forests. True birds flew in the air, true snakes crawled upon the ground, and in the waters were whales and many kinds of fishes of the present day. But the marine monsters and the gigantic and ferocious saurians of an earlier age had disappeared. So the world became fitted to be the dwelling-place of the human race. Then began the age of Man, an age which is yet not complete.

Such, in brief, is the history of the earth as the rocks have told it to us. Without their help we could know but little of the story. Through all the periods of time and all the ages, they were being formed, layer upon layer, of sand and silt, of mud and pebbles, hardening with the pass-

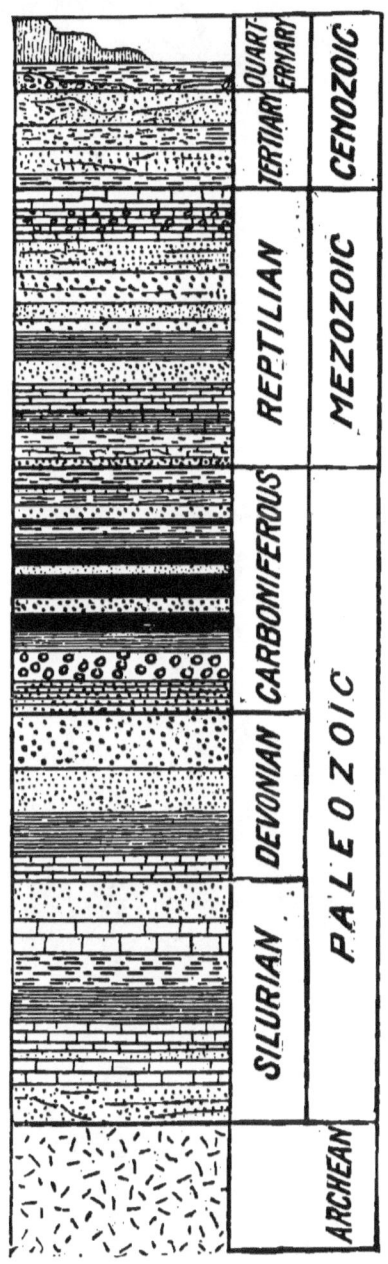

COLUMNAR SECTION OF THE
EARTH'S CRUST.

ing of the centuries. But while they were still soft they received impressions of the feet of birds and of beasts, they were marked by the waves and were cracked in the fierce heat of the sun, and their surfaces were pitted by the rain-drops of passing showers. Shells, corals, and sponges were imbedded in them; the skeletons of fishes and the bones of animals that walked or crept upon the land or flew in the air were covered over by them; they caught and held the drooping fern, the falling leaf and twig and nut; they closed around the body of the tree itself and buried it from sight; and as the soil hardened into rock, bone and shell, leaf and stem, hardened with it and became part of it. To-day we find these fossil remains, sometimes near the surface of the earth, sometimes hundreds or thousands of feet below it. We uncover them from the soil, we break them from the rock, we blast them out in the quarries, we dig them from the mines of coal and ore. It is by them and by the structure of the rock which contains them that we read the history of the earth, a history covering so long a period of time from the beginning of the stratification of the rocks to the age when man appeared upon the globe that no one has yet dared to reckon the millions upon millions of years which intervened, and give the result of his computation to the world as true.

CHAPTER II.

THE COMPOSITION OF COAL.

THE first question that would naturally be asked concerning the subject with which we are dealing is, What is coal?

In reply it may be said that it is a mineral. It is black or brown in color, solid, heavy, and amorphous. The specific gravity of the average Pennsylvania anthracite is about 1.6, and of the bituminous coal about 1.4. There are four varieties of mineral coal, namely: anthracite, bituminous, lignite or brown coal, and cannel coal. To this list it would not be improper to add peat, since it partakes of most of the characteristics of mineral coal, and would doubtless develop into such coal if the process of transformation were allowed to continue undisturbed. The principal element contained in each of these different kinds of coal is carbon. An analysis of an average piece of Pennsylvania anthracite would show the following chemical composition:—

Fixed carbon	86.4
Ash	6.2
Water	3.7
Volatile matter	3.1
Sulphur	.6
Total	100

THE COMPOSITION OF COAL.

The composition of the bituminous coals of Pennsylvania, as represented by the gas coal of Westmoreland County, is shown by analysis to be as follows: —

Fixed carbon	55.
Volatile matter	37.5
Ash	5.4
Water	1.4
Sulphur	.7
Total	100

An analysis of coal from the Pittsburgh region would show its percentage of carbon to be from 58 to 64, and of volatile matter and ash to be proportionately less.

There is no strict line of demarcation between the anthracite and the bituminous coals. They are classed generally, according to the amount of carbon and volatile matter contained in them, as: —

Hard-dry Anthracites,
Semi-Anthracite,
Semi-Bituminous,
Bituminous.

Coals of the first class contain from 91 to 98 per cent. of carbon, and of the second class from 85 to 90 per cent. The volatile matter in the third class is usually less than 18 per cent., and in the fourth class more than 18 per cent. of its composition.

The anthracite coal is hard and brittle, and has a rich black color and a metallic lustre. It ignites with difficulty, and at first burns with a small blue flame of carbonic oxide. This disappears, however, when ignition is complete. No smoke is given off during combustion. Semi-anthracite coal is neither so hard, so dense, nor so brilliant in lustre as the anthracite, though when once fully ignited it has all the characteristic features of the latter in combustion. It is found principally at the western ends of the anthracite coal basins.

Bituminous coal is usually deep black in color, with little or no lustre, having planes of cleavage which run nearly at right angles with each other, so that when the coal is broken it separates into cubical fragments. It ignites easily and burns with a yellowish flame. It gives off smoke and leaves a large percentage of ashes after combustion. That variety of it known as caking or coking coal is the most important. This is quite soft, and will not bear much handling. During combustion it swells, fuses, and finally runs together in large porous masses.

Following the question of the composition of coal comes the question of its origin, of which, indeed, there is no longer any serious doubt. It is generally conceded that coal is a vegetable product, and there are excellent reasons for this belief. The fragments of which coal is composed have been greatly deformed by compression and decomposition. But when one of those fragments is made so thin that it will transmit light, and is then subjected to a powerful microscope, its vegetable structure may readily be distinguished; that is, the fragments are seen to be the fragments of plants. Immediately under every separate seam of coal there is a stratum of what is known as fire clay. It may, under the beds of softer coals, be of the consistency of clay; but under the coal seams of the harder varieties it is usually in the form of a slaty rock. This fire clay stratum is always present, and contains in great abundance the fossil impressions of roots and stems and twigs, showing that it was once the soil from which vegetation grew luxuriantly. It is common also to find fossil tree-stems lying mashed flat between the layers of black slate which form the roof of the coal mines, also the impressions of the leaves, nuts, and seeds which fell from these trees while they were living. In some beds of cannel coal whole trees have been found, with roots, branches, leaves, and seeds complete, and all converted into the same quality of coal by which they were surrounded. In short, the strata of the coal measures everywhere are full of the fossil impressions of plants, of great variety both in kind and size.

If a piece of wood be subjected to heat and great pressure, a substance is obtained which strongly resembles mineral coal.

That coal contains a very large proportion of carbon in its composition has already been noted. If, therefore, it is a vegetable product, the vegetation from which it was formed must have been subjected to some process by which a large part of its substance was eliminated, since wood or woody fibre contains only from 20 to 25 per cent. of carbon. But wood can be transformed, by combustion, into charcoal, a material containing in its composition 98 per cent. of carbon, or a greater percentage than the best anthracite contains. This cannot be done, however, by burning wood in an open fire, for in that case its carbon unites with atmospheric oxygen and passes invisibly into the air. It must be subjected to a process of smothered combustion; free access of air must be denied to it while it is burning. Then the volatile matter will be freed and expelled, and, since the carbon cannot come in contact with the oxygen of the air, it will be retained, together with a small percentage of ash. The result will be charcoal, or coal artificially made. The principle on which this transformation is based is combustion or decomposition out of contact with atmospheric air. But Nature is as familiar with this principle as is man, and she may not only be discovered putting it in practice, but the entire process may be watched from beginning to end. One must go, for this purpose, first, to a peat bed. This is simply an accumulation of the remains of plants which grew and decayed on the spot where they are now found. As these remains were deposited each year, every layer became buried under its succeeding layer, until finally a great thickness was obtained. When we remove the upper layer we find peat with its 52 to 66 per cent. of carbon, and the deeper we go the better is the quality of the substance. It may be cut out in blocks with sharp spades, the water may be pressed from the blocks, and they may be stacked up, covered and dried, and used for fuel. In most peat bogs the process of growth is going on, and may be watched. There is a certain kind of moss called *sphagnum*, which in large part makes up the peat-producing vegetation. Its roots die annually, but from the living top new roots are sent out each year. The workmen who dig peat understand that if this surface is destroyed the growth of the bed must stop; consequently in many instances they have removed the sod carefully, and after taking out a stratum of peat have replaced the sod in order that the bed may be renewed. There is little doubt that if these beds of peat could lie undisturbed and covered over through many ages they would take on all the characteristics of mineral coal.

A step farther back in geological history we reach the period of the latest formations of lignite or brown coal. This coal is first found in the strata of the glacial period, or first period in the age of Man. But it is found there in an undeveloped state. The woody fibre has not yet undergone the complete transformation into coal. The trunks and branches of trees have indeed become softened to the consistence of soap, but they still retain their natural color. Going back, however, to the strata of the Miocene or second period of the Tertiary age or age of Mammals, we find that this wood has become black, though it has not yet hardened. But when we reach the upper cretaceous or last period of the age of Reptiles, the transformation into coal has become complete. The woody fibre is now black, hard, and compact, though it may still be easily disaggregated by atmospheric action, and we have the true lignite, so called because of its apparent woody structure.

The next step takes us back to the bituminous coal of the Carboniferous age, the character and consistency of which has already been noted, and finally we reach the complete development in anthracite. It is, however, the opinion of the best geologists that the bituminous and anthracite coals are of the same age, and were originally of the same formation and character. That is, they were all bituminous; but during the violent contortions and upheavals of the earth's crust at the time of the Appalachian revolution at the close of the Carboniferous age, the bituminous coals involved in that disturbance were changed by heat, pressure, and motion, and the consequent expulsion of volatile matter, from bituminous to anthracite.

Cannel coal is a variety of bituminous coal, burning with great freedom, the flame of which affords considerable light. It was called "candle coal" by the English people who first used it, as it often served as a substitute for that household necessity. But the name soon became corrupted to "cannel," and has so remained. It is duller and more compact than the ordinary bituminous coal, and it can be wrought in a lathe and polished. A certain variety of it, found in the lower oölitic strata of Yorkshire in England, is manufactured into a kind of jewelry, well known by its popular name of *jet*.

CHAPTER III.

WHEN COAL WAS FORMED.

It becomes of interest now to examine briefly into the causes and process of the transformation from vegetable substance into coal, to note the character of the vegetation which went to make up the coal beds, and to glance at the animal life of the period.

As has already been said, the plants of the Carboniferous age were exceedingly abundant and luxuriant. They grew up richly from the clayey soil, and formed dense jungles in the vast marshes which covered so large an area of the earth's surface. Ferns, mosses, and tufts of surface vegetation, and the leaves, branches, and trunks of trees fell and decayed on the place where they grew, only to make the soil more fertile and the next growth richer and more luxuriant. Year after year, century after century, this process of growth and decay went on, until the beds of vegetable matter thus deposited had reached a great thickness. But condensation was still in progress in the earth's body, and in consequence of it her crust, of necessity, at times contracted and fell. When it did so the land sank throughout vast areas, these beds of incipient coal went down, and over the great marshes the waters swept again, bringing drift of vegetation from higher levels to add to that already buried. Then over these deposits of vegetable matter the sand and mud and gravel were laid up anew, and the clayey soil from which the next rich growth should spring was spread out upon the surface. This process was repeated again and again, as often, indeed, as we find seams of coal in any coal bed. Thus the final condition for the formation of coal was met, the exclusion of atmospheric air from this mass of decaying vegetation was complete, and under the water of the ocean, under the sand and silt of the shore, under the new deposits of succeeding ages, the transformation went on, the wood of the Carboniferous era became the coal of to-day, while above and below it the sand and clay were hardened into rock and shale.

The remarkable features of the vegetation of the coal era were the size and abundance of its plants. Trees of that time whose trunks were from one to three feet in diameter, and which grew to a height of from forty to one hundred feet, are represented in our day by mere stems a fraction of an inch in diameter and but one or two feet high. A comparison of quantity would show differences as great as does the comparison of size.

But at that time all the conditions were favorable for the rapid and enormous growth of vegetation. The air was laden with carbon, which is the principal food for plants; so laden, indeed, that man, who is eminently an oxygen-breathing animal, could not have lived in it. The great humidity of the atmosphere was another element favorable to growth. Vegetation never lacked for an abundance of moisture either at root or leaf. Then, too, the climate was universally warm. Over the entire surface of the earth the heat was greater than it is to-day at the torrid zone. It must be remembered that the internal fires of the globe have been constantly cooling and receding, and that the earth, in the Carboniferous age, was subjected to the greater power of a larger sun than shines upon us to-day.

With all these circumstances in its favor, warmth, moisture, and an atmosphere charged heavily with carbon, vegetation could not help but flourish. That it did flourish amazingly is abundantly shown by its fossil remains. The impressions of more than five hundred different species of plants that grew in the Carboniferous era have been found in the coal measures. There are few of them that bear any direct analogy to existing species, and these few have their counterparts only in the torrid zone. The most abundant of the plants of the coal era were the ferns. Their fossil remains are found in great profusion and variety in most of the rocks of the coal-bearing strata. There was also the plant known as the tree fern, which attained a height of twenty or thirty feet and carried a single tuft of leaves radiating from its top. Probably the species next in abundance, as it certainly is next in importance, to the ferns is that of the Lepidodendrids. It doubtless contributed the greatest proportion of woody material to the composition of coal. The plants of this species were forest trees, but are supposed to have been analogous to the low club mosses of the present. Fossil trunks of Lepidodendrids have been found measuring from one hundred to one hundred and thirty feet in length, and from six to ten feet in diameter.

Similar in appearance to the Lepidodendrids were the Sigillariæ, which were also very abundant. The Conifers were of quite a different species from those already named, and probably grew on higher ground. They were somewhat analogous to the modern pine.

The Calamites belonged to the horsetail family. They grew up with long, reed-like, articulated stems to a height of twenty feet or more, and with a diameter of ten or twelve inches. They stood close together in the muddy ground, forming an almost impenetrable thicket, and probably made up a very large percentage of the vegetation which was transformed into coal.

One of the most abundant species of plants of the coal era is that of Stigmaria. Stout stems, from two to four inches in diameter, branched downward from a short trunk, and then grew out in long root-like processes, floating in the water or trailing on the mud to distances of twenty or thirty feet. These are the roots with which the under clay of every coal seam is usually filled.

The plants which have been described, together with their kindred species, formed the largest and most important part of the vegetation of the Carboniferous age. But of the hundreds of varieties which then abounded, the greater portion reached their highest stage of perfection in the coal era, and became extinct before the close of Paleozoic time. Other types were lost during Mesozoic time, and to-day there is scarcely a counterpart in existence of any of the multitude of forms of plant life that grew and flourished in that far-off age of the world.

The animal life of the Carboniferous era was confined almost entirely to the water. The dry land had not yet begun to produce in abundance the higher forms of living things. There were spiders there, however, and scorpions, and centipedes, and even cockroaches. There were also land snails, beetles, locusts, and mayflies. Reptiles, with clumsy feet and dragging tails, prowled about on the wet sands of the shore, leaving footprints that were never effaced by time or the elements, and are found to-day in the layers of the rocks, almost as perfect as when they were formed, millions of years ago. But the waters teemed with animal life. On the bottom of the shallow seas lay shells and corals in such abundance and variety that from the deposits of their remains great beds of limestone have been formed. Broken into minute fragments by the action of the waves and washed up by the sea during periods of submergence, they were spread over the beds of carboniferous deposits, and became the rock strata through which the drills and shafts of to-day are sunk to reach the veins of mineral coal.

Fishes were numerous. Some of them, belonging to species allied to the modern shark, were of great size, with huge fin spines fully eighteen inches in length. These spines have been found as fossils, as have also the scales, teeth, and bones. Complete skeletons of smaller fishes of the ganoid order were preserved in the rock as it hardened, and now form fossil specimens which are unequaled in beauty and perfection.

Besides the fishes, there were the swimming reptiles; amphibian monsters, allied to the ichthyosaurs and plesiosaurs which were so abundant during the Reptilian age that followed. These animals are known as enaliosaurs. They attained great size, being from twenty-five to fifty feet in length; they had air-breathing apparatus, and propelled themselves through the water with paddles like the paddles of whales. Their enormous jaws were lined with rows of sharp, pointed teeth, and their food was fish, shell-fish, and any other kind of animal life that came within their reach. They devoured even their own species. Living mostly in the open seas or fresh-water lagoons, they sometimes chased their prey far up the rivers, and sometimes basked in the sunshine on the sands of the shore. Frightful in aspect, fierce, and voracious, they were the terror and the tyrants of the seas.

Such were the animals, such were the plants, that lived and died, that flourished and decayed, in the age when coal was being formed and fashioned and hidden away in the crust of the earth. That the fauna and flora of to-day have few prototypes among them should be little cause for regret. There was, indeed, hardly a feature in the landscape of the coal era that would have had a familiar look to an inhabitant of the world in its present age. In place of the hills and valleys as we have them now, there were great plains sloping imperceptibly to the borders of the sea. There were vast marshes, shallow fresh-water lakes, and broad and sluggish rivers. Save by isolated peaks the Rocky Mountains had not yet been uplifted from the face of the deep, and the great West of to-day was a waste of waters. In the wide forests no bird's song was ever heard, no flashing of a wing was ever seen, no serpent trailed its length upon the ground, no wild beast searched the woods for prey. The spider spun his web in silence from the dew-wet twigs, the locust hopped drowsily from leaf to leaf, the mayfly floated lightly in the heavy air, the slow-paced snail left his damp track on the surfaces of the rocks, and the beetles, lifting the hard coverings from their gauzy wings, flew aimlessly from place to place. In seas and lakes and swampy pools strange fishes swam, up from the salt waters odd reptiles crawled to sun themselves upon the sandy shore or make their way through the dense jungles of the swamps, and out where the ocean waves were dashing, fierce monsters of the sea darted on their prey, or churned the water into foam in savage fights with each other.

But in all the world there were no flowers. Stems grew to be trunks, branches were sent out, leaves formed and fell, the land was robed and wrapped in the richest, most luxuriant foliage, yet the few buds that tried to blossom were scentless and hidden, and earth was still void of the beauty and the fragrance of the flowers.

CHAPTER IV.

HOW THE COAL BEDS LIE.

THE process of growth, deposition, submergence, and burial, described in the preceding chapter, continued throughout the Carboniferous age. Each period of inundation and of the covering over of beds of vegetable deposit by sand and silt is marked by the layers of stratified rock that intervene between, and that overlie the separate seams of coal in the coal measures of to-day. The number of these coal seams indicates the number of periods during which the growth and decay of vegetation was uninterrupted. This number, in the anthracite coal regions, varies from ten to thirty or thereabouts, but in the bituminous regions it scarcely ever exceeds eight or ten. The thickness of the separate coal seams also varies greatly, ranging from a fraction of an inch up to sixty or seventy feet. Indeed, there are basins of small extent in the south of France and in India where the seam is two hundred feet thick. It is seldom, however, that workable seams of anthracite exceed twenty feet in thickness, and by far the largest number of them do not go above eight or ten, while the seams of bituminous coal do not even average these last figures in thickness. Neither is the entire thickness of a seam made up of pure coal. Bands of slate called "partings" usually run horizontally through a seam, dividing it into "benches." These partings vary from a fraction of an inch to several feet in thickness, and make up from one fifth to one seventh of the entire seam.

The rock strata between the coal seams range from three feet to three hundred feet in thickness, and in exceptional cases go as high as five or six hundred feet. Perhaps a fair average would be from eighty to one hundred feet. These rock intervals are made up mostly of sandstones and shales. The combined average thickness of the coal seams of Pennsylvania varies from twenty-five feet at Pittsburgh in the western bituminous region to one hundred and twenty feet at Pottsville in the eastern anthracite district, and may be said to average about one fiftieth of the entire thickness of the coal measures, which is placed at 4,000 feet.

Some conception may be had of the enormous vegetable deposits of the Carboniferous era by recalling the fact that the resultant coal in each seam is only from one ninth to one sixteenth in bulk of the woody fibre from which it has been derived, the loss being mainly in oxygen and hydrogen. It is probable that the coal seams as well as the rock strata had attained a comparative degree of hardness before the close of the Carboniferous age. It was at the close of this age that those profound disturbances of the earth's crust throughout eastern North America took place which have already been referred to. Hitherto, through the long ages of Paleozoic time, there had been comparative quiet. As cooling and contraction of the earth's body were still going on, there were doubtless oscillations of surface and subsidence of strata in almost continuous progress. But these movements were very slow, amounting, perhaps, to not more than a foot in a century. Yet in Pennsylvania and Virginia the sinking of the crust up to the close of the Carboniferous age amounted to 35,000 or 40,000 feet. That the subsidence was quiet and unmarked by violent movement is attested by the regularity of strata, especially of the carboniferous measures, which alone show a sinking of 3,000 or 4,000 feet. Neither were the disturbances which followed violent, nor were the changes paroxysmal. Indeed, the probability is that they took place gradually through long periods of time. They were, nevertheless, productive of enormous results in the shape of hills, peaks, and mountain ranges. These movements in the earth's crust were due, as always, to contractions in the earth's body or reductions in its bulk. On the same principle by which the skin of an apple that has dried without decay is thrown into folds and wrinkles, the earth's crust became corrugated. There is this difference, however: the crust, being hard and unyielding, has often been torn and broken in the process of change. Naturally these ridges in the earth's surface have been lifted along the lines of least resistance, and these lines seem to have been, at the time of the Appalachian revolution, practically parallel to the line of the Atlantic coast, though long spurs were thrown out in other directions, isolated dome-shaped elevations were raised up, and bowl-shaped valleys were hollowed out among the hills.

The anthracite coal beds were in the regions of greatest disturbance, and, together with the rock strata above and below them, assumed new positions, which were inclined at all angles to their old ones of horizontality. More than this, the heat and pressure of that period exerted upon these beds of coal, which up to this time had been bituminous in character, resulted in the expulsion of so large a portion of the volatile matter still remaining in them as to change their character from bituminous to anthracite. Although the strata, in the positions to which they have been forced, are at times broken and abrupt, yet as a rule they rise and fall in wave-like folds or ridges. These ridges are called *anticlinals*, because the strata slope in opposite directions from a common plane. The valleys between the ridges are called *synclinals*, because the strata slope from opposite directions toward a common plane. One result of this great force of compression exerted on the earth's crust was to make rents in it across the lines of strata. These rents are called *fissures*. Sometimes the faces of a fissure are parallel and sometimes they inclose a wedge-shaped cavity. This cavity, whatever its shape, is usually filled either with igneous rock that has come up from the molten mass below, or with surface drift or broken rock fragments that have been deposited there from above. Where there is displacement as well as fracture, that is when the strata on one side of a fissure have been pushed up or have fallen below the corresponding strata on the other side, we have what is known as a *fault*. Sometimes the displacement seems to have been accomplished with little disturbance to the sides of the fissure; at other times we find, along the line of fracture, evidences of great destruction caused by the pushing up of strata in this way. A fault may reach a comparatively short distance, or it may traverse a country for miles. The vertical displacement may be only a few inches, or it may amount to hundreds or thousands of feet. In the bituminous coal regions, where the strata lie comparatively undisturbed, faults are but little known. In the anthracite districts they are common, but not great.

Besides the great folds into which the earth's crust was crowded, there are usually smaller folds

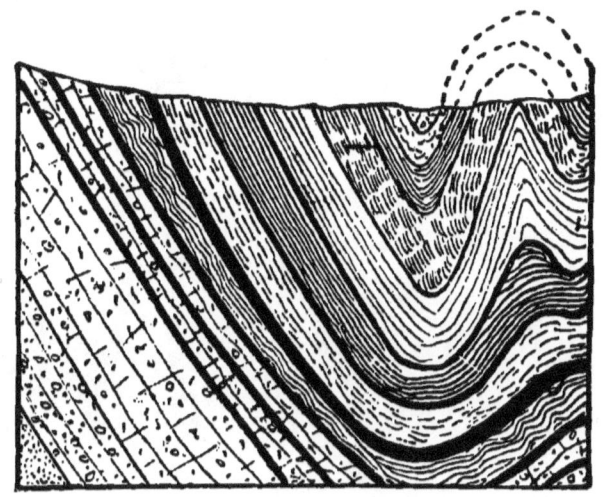

VERTICAL SECTION THROUGH SOUTHERN COAL FIELD.

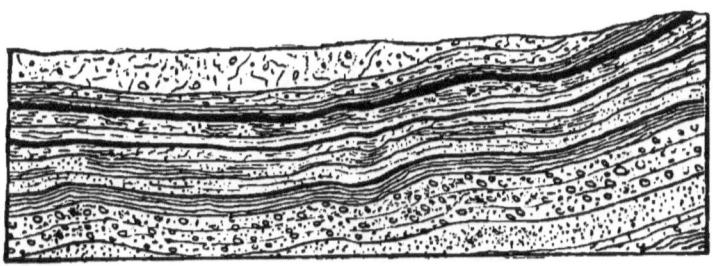

VERTICAL SECTION THROUGH NORTHERN COAL FIELD.

corrugating the slopes of the greater ones, sometimes running parallel with them, oftener stretching across them at various angles. A marked instance of this formation is found in the Wyoming coal basin, the general coal bed of which is in the shape of a canoe, about fifty miles long, from two to six miles broad, and with a maximum depth of perhaps one thousand feet. Running diagonally across this basin, in practically parallel lines from one extremity to the other, is a series of gentle anticlinals, dividing the basin into some thirty smaller synclinal valleys or sub-basins.

The irregularities produced by folds, fissures, faults, and partings are not the only ones with which the miner has to deal. So far we have supposed the coal seams to have been laid down in horizontal layers of uniform thickness, with smooth and regular under and upper surfaces. This is true only in a large sense. As a matter of fact each separate seam varies greatly in thickness, and its roof and floor are often broken and irregular. The beds of clay on which the deposits were laid were pushed up unevenly by the exuberant growth of vegetation from them. The action of waves and ocean currents made hollows in them, and laid down ridges and mounds of sand on them, around and over which the decaying vegetation rose and hardened. The same forces, together with the action of running streams, made channels and hollows in the upper surfaces of these beds of incipient coal, which cavities became filled by sand and gravel, and this also hardened into rock. These irregularities are found by the miner of to-day in the floor and roof of the coal seam, and are called *rolls, horses,* or *horse-backs.* When the coal seam thins out so rapidly that the floor and roof come nearly together, this state of things is called a *pinch,* or *squeeze,* though the latter term is more properly applied to the settling of the roof rock after the coal has been mined out. The inequalities of a coal seam that have now been mentioned, although perhaps but a small portion of those that are daily met with in the process of mining, are neverthless characteristic of the whole.

The hills and mountain ranges that were thrown up at the close of the Carboniferous age were many times higher and broader then than they are to-day. Heat and cold and the storms of a thousand centuries, working by disintegration and erosion, have worn away their substance, the valleys and low lands are filled with it, and the rivers are always carrying it down to the sea. The peaks and the crests have been the portions of the elevations that have suffered most. It is often as though the tops of the anticlinal folds had been sliced off for the purpose of filling the valleys with them to the level of the decapitated hills. A great part of the coal measures have thus wasted away; in some portions of the anthracite district by far the greater part, including many valuable coal seams.

HOW THE COAL BEDS LIE.

When a fold or flexure of the earth's crust has been decapitated in the manner mentioned, the exposed edge of any stratum of rock or coal is called its *outcrop*. The angle of inclination at which any stratum descends into the earth is called its *dip*. The direction of a horizontal line drawn along the face of a stratum of rock or coal is its *strike*. It is obvious that the strike must always be at right angles to the dip. That is, if the dip is downward toward the east or toward the west, the direction of the strike must be north and south. It is now apparent that if one begins at the outcrop of a coal seam and traces the course of the seam downward along the line of dip, his path will lie down the inclination for a longer or shorter distance, until the bottom of the synclinal valley is reached. This is known as the *basin* or *swamp*. Here the seam may be comparatively level for a short distance; more often it has a mild vertical curve, and starts up the dip on the other side of the valley, which inclination may be followed till the outcrop is reached. If now the decapitated portion of the fold could be replaced in its natural position, we could trace the same seam up to and over the anticlinal axis and down upon the other side. As it is, we must cross on the surface from the outcrop to the place where the corresponding seam enters the earth. In the southern and eastern anthracite coal districts of Pennsylvania decapitation of folds to a point below the coal measures is general; the coal seams dip into the earth with a very sharp pitch, and the coal basins are often very deep and very narrow, striking into the earth almost like a wedge. In the northern or Wyoming district decapitation is not so general, the angle of inclination of strata is mild, and the basins are wide and comparatively shallow. In the bituminous districts, where the disturbance to the earth's crust has been slight, the coal beds lie very nearly as they were formed, the dip seldom exceeding an angle of five degrees with the horizon. The exposures here are due generally to the erosive action of water.

The carboniferous measures are the highest and latest geological formation in the great coal fields of the United States. Therefore where the strata have not been disturbed by flexure the coal seams lie near the surface. This is generally the case in the bituminous districts, and it is also partially true in the northern anthracite coal field. Deep mining is necessary only in the middle and southern anthracite coal fields, where the folds are close and precipitous, and the deep and narrow basins formed by them have been filled with deposits of a later geologic age.

Some of the difficulties to be met and overcome in mining coal will by this time have been appreciated by the reader. But some of them only. The inequalities of roof and floor, the pitching seams, the folds and faults and fissures, all the

OLD OPENING INTO AN OUT-CROP OF THE BALTIMORE VEIN.

accidents and irregularities of formation and of location, make up but a few of the problems which face the mining engineer. But the intellect and ingenuity of men have overcome most of the obstacles which Nature placed in the way of successful mining when she hardened the rocks above her coal beds, crowded the earth's crust into folds, and lifted the mountain ranges into the air.

It will not be out of place at this time to make mention of those localities in which coal is found. Indeed, there are few countries on the globe in which there are not carboniferous deposits of greater or less extent. Great Britain, with Ireland, has about 12,000 square miles of them. In England alone there is an area of 8,139 square miles of workable coal beds. In continental Europe the coal fields are numerous, but the character of the deposit is inferior. Coal is found also in the Asiatic countries, in Australia, and in South America; and in Nova Scotia and New Brunswick there is an area of 18,000 square miles of coal measures. The combined areas of coal measures in the United States amount to about 185,000 square miles. The Appalachian or Alleghany region contains about 60,000 square miles, included in the States of Pennsylvania, Virginia, West Virginia, Maryland, Ohio, Kentucky, Tennessee, Georgia, and Alabama. The Illinois and Missouri region contains also about 60,000 square miles, and has areas not only in the States named, but also in Indiana, Iowa, Kentucky, Kansas, and Arkansas. Michigan has about 5,000 and Rhode Island about 500 square miles. There are also small areas in Utah and Texas, and in the far West there are workable coal fields in Colorado, Dakota, Indian Territory, Montana, New Mexico, Washington, Wyoming Territory, Oregon, and California. The entire coal area of the United States, with the exception of that in Rhode Island and a few outlying sections in Pennsylvania, contains coal of the bituminous variety only. Both the area and supply are therefore practically without limit. In the coal regions of Rhode Island the disturbances affecting the earth's crust have been very violent. The motion, heat, and compression have been so great as to give the rocks associated with the coal measures a true metamorphic or crystalline structure, and to transform the coal itself into an extremely hard anthracite; in some places, indeed, it has been altered to graphite. The flexures of the coal formation are very abrupt and full of faults, and the coal itself is greatly broken and displaced. Its condition is such that it cannot be mined with great profit, and but little of it is now sent to market. The only areas of readily workable anthracite in the United States are therefore in Pennsylvania. These are all east of the Alleghany Mountains, and are located in four distinct regions. The first or Southern Coal Field extends from the

HOW THE COAL BEDS LIE. 33

Lehigh River at Mauch Chunk, southwest to within a few miles of the Susquehanna River, ending at this extremity in the form of a fish's tail. It is seventy-five miles in length, averages somewhat less than two miles in breadth, and has an area of one hundred and forty square miles. It lies in Carbon, Schuylkill, and Dauphin counties. The second or Western Middle field, known also as the Mahanoy and Shamokin field, lies between the eastern headwaters of the Little Schuylkill River and the Susquehanna River. It has an area of about ninety square miles, and is situated in the counties of Schuylkill, Columbia, and Northumberland. It lies just north of the Southern field, and the two together are frequently spoken of as the Schuylkill Region. The Eastern Middle or Upper Lehigh field lies northeast of the first two fields, and is separated into nine distinct parallel canoe-shaped basins. These extend from the Lehigh River on the east to the Catawissa Creek on the west, and comprise an area of about forty miles. They are principally in Luzerne County, but extend also into Carbon, Schuylkill, and Columbia counties. The Northern or Wyoming field is a crescent-shaped basin about fifty miles long and from two to six miles broad, with an area of about two hundred square miles. Its westerly cusp is just north of the Eastern Middle field, and it extends from that point northeasterly through Luzerne and Lackawanna counties, just cutting into Wayne and Susquehanna counties with its northern cusp. It lies in the valleys of the Susquehanna and Lackawanna rivers, and in it are situated the mining towns of Plymouth, Wilkes Barre, Pittston, Scranton, and Carbondale. There is also a fifth district, known as the Loyalsock and Mehoopany coal field, lying in Sullivan and Wyoming counties. It is from twenty to twenty-five miles northwest of the Wyoming and Lackawanna field, its area is limited, and its coals are not true anthracite.

It will thus be seen that aside from this last field the anthracite coal area of Pennsylvania contains about four hundred and seventy square miles.

CHAPTER V.

THE DISCOVERY OF COAL.

ALTHOUGH it has been within comparatively recent times that coal has come into general use as a fuel, yet there can be no doubt that it was discovered, and that its qualities were known, many centuries ago. To prove its use by the ancients, mention is sometimes made of a passage from the writings of Theophrastus, a pupil and friend of Aristotle and for many years the head of the peripatetic school of philosophy. This passage dates back to about 300 B. C., and is as follows: "Those substances that are called coals and are broken for use are earthy, but they kindle and burn like wooden coals. They are found in Liguria where there is amber, and in Elis over the mountains toward Olympus. They are used by the smiths."

The word "coal," however, as used in the Bible and other ancient books, usually means charcoal, or burning wood. It is claimed, and not without plausibility, that coal was mined in Britain prior to the Roman invasion. The cinder heaps found among ruins of the time of Roman supremacy in the island point to quite an extensive use of coal by the people of that age. But no writings have been found recording the use of coal prior to 852 A. D. In that year twelve cartloads of "fossil fuel," or "pit coal," were received by the abbey of Peterborough in England, and the receipt was recorded. It is said that coal first began to be systematically mined in Great Britain about the year 1180.

It is certain that by the end of the thirteenth century the exportation of coal from Newcastle was considerable, and the new fuel had come to be largely used in London. But the people of that city conceived the idea that its use was injurious to the health of the inhabitants generally. The coal, being of the bituminous variety, burned with considerable flame and gave off a good deal of smoke, and the ignorance of the people led them into the belief that the air was contaminated and poisoned by the products of combustion. So they presented a petition to Parliament asking that the burning of coal be prohibited in the city of London. Not only was the prayer of the petitioners granted, but in order to render the prohibition effectual an act was passed making it a capital offense to burn the dreaded fuel. This was in the reign of Edward I., and is characteristic of the policy of that strong, unyielding king, whose ends, great and just perhaps, were too often attained by harsh and cruel means.

The coal industry was checked, but it was not

destroyed; for, half a century later, we find Edward III. granting a license to the inhabitants of Newcastle " to dig coals and stones in the common soil of the town without the walls thereof in the place called the Castle Field and the Forth." Afterward this town, owing to the fine coal beds in its vicinity, became one of the great centres of the British coal trade, from which fact doubtless arose that ancient saying concerning useless trouble or labor, that it is like " carrying coals to Newcastle."

In Scotland coal was mined in the twelfth century and in Germany in the thirteenth, and the Chinese had already become familiar with its use. But in Paris the same prejudice was excited against it that had prevailed in London, and it did not come into use in that city as a household fuel until about the middle of the sixteenth century. This was also the date of its introduction into Wales, Belgium, and other European countries.

That coal was familiar, in appearance at least, to the natives of America, long before the feet of white men ever pressed American soil, cannot well be doubted. They must have seen it at its numerous outcrops; perhaps they took pieces of it in their hard hands, handled it, broke it, powdered it, or cast it away from them as useless. Indeed, it is not improbable that they should have known something of its qualities as a fuel. But of this there is no proof. The first record we have of the observation of coal in this country was made by Father Hennepin, a French explorer, in 1679. On a map of his explorations he marked the site of a coal mine on the bank of the Illinois River above Fort Crevecœur, near the present town of Ottawa. In his record of travel he states that in the country then occupied by the Pimitoui or Pimitwi Indians "there are mines of coal, slate, and iron." The oldest coal workings in America are doubtless those in what is known as the Richmond or Chesterfield coal bed, near Richmond in Chesterfield and Powhatan counties in the State of Virginia. It is supposed that coal was discovered and mined there as early as 1750. But by whom and under what circumstances the discovery was made we have only tradition to inform us. This says that one day, during the year last named, a certain boy, living in that vicinity, went out into an unfrequented district on a private and personal fishing excursion. Either the fish bit better than he had thought they would, or for some other cause his supply of bait ran out, and it became necessary for him to renew it. Hunting around in the small creeks and inlets for crawfish with which to bait his hook, he chanced to stumble upon the outcrop of a coal bed which crosses the James River about twelve miles above Richmond. He made his discovery known, and further examination disclosed a seam of rich bituminous coal, which has since been conceded to be a formation of Mesozoic time rather than of the Carboniferous age. Mining operations were soon begun, and were carried on so successfully that by the year 1775 the coal was in general use in the vicinity for smithing and domestic purposes. It played a part in the war for independence by entering into the manufacture of cannon balls, and by 1789 it had achieved so much of a reputation that it was being shipped to Philadelphia, New York, and Boston, and sold in those markets. But the mines were operated by slave labor, and mining was carried on in the most primitive fashion for three quarters of a century. So late as 1860 the improved systems of mining, long in use in the North, were still comparatively unknown at the Virginia mines.

During the war of the rebellion these mines were seized by the Confederate government and operated by it, in order to obtain directly the necessary fuel for purposes of modern warfare; and upon the cessation of hostilities the paralysis which had fallen upon all other Southern industries fell also upon this. But with the revival of business, mining was again begun in the Richmond field, and from 1874 to the present time the industry has prospered and grown, and Virginia has furnished to the country at large a considerable amount of an excellent quality of bituminous coal. This coal bed covers an area of about 180 square miles, and has an average thickness of twenty-four feet. It is supposed to contain about 50,000,000 of tons yet unmined.

Another of the early discoveries of coal in the United States was that of the Rhode Island anthracite bed in 1760. Mines began to be regularly worked here in 1808, but only about 750,000 tons, all told, have been taken from them. For reasons which have been already given these mines cannot be profitably worked in competition with the anthracite mines of Pennsylvania, in which the location and formation of the coal beds are greatly superior.

It is impossible to say when the coal of the great bituminous district of Pennsylvania and Ohio was first seen by white men. In the summer of 1755 General Braddock led his army through western Pennsylvania by a military road to that terrible defeat and slaughter in which he himself received his death wound. This road, laid out by the army's engineers and graded by its men, was so well built that its course can still be traced, and it is seen to have crossed the outcrop of the Pittsburgh coal seam in many places. It is not improbable that a large number of the soldiers in the English army were familiar with the appearance of coal, and knew how to mine it and use it. Indeed, Colonel James Burd, who was engaged in the construction of the road, claims to have burned about a bushel of this coal on his camp-fire at that time.

Some of the English soldiers who survived that terrible disaster to their arms afterward returned and purchased lands in the vicinity, and it is reasonable to suppose that the coal was dug and put to use by them. A lease, still in existence, dated April 11, 1767, making a grant of lands on "Coal Pitt Creek," in Westmoreland County, indicates that there were coal openings there at that date. Captain Thomas Hutchins, who visited Fort Pitt (now Pittsburgh) in 1760, mentions the fact that he found an open coal mine on the opposite side of the Monongahela River, from which coal was being taken for the use of the garrison.

From 1770 to 1777 it was common for maps of certain portions of the Ohio River country to have marked on them sites of coal beds along the shores of that stream in regions which are now known to contain seams of the great bituminous deposit.

Probably the Susquehanna River region was the first in which this coal was dug systematically and put to use. It was burned by blacksmiths in their forges, and as early as 1785 the river towns were supplied with it by Samuel Boyd, who shipped it from his mines in arks. In 1813 Philip Karthaus took a quantity of coal to Fort Deposit, and sent it thence by canal to Philadelphia. After this he sent cargoes regularly to Philadelphia and Baltimore, and sold them readily at the rate of thirty-three cents per bushel. This trade was stopped, however, by the building of dams across the Susquehanna, and it was not until many years afterward that the mineral resources of this section of the coal field were developed again through the introduction of railroads.

In the Pittsburgh region the demand for coal increased with the increase of population, and at the beginning of the present century it was in general use, not only in the manufacturing industries but also as a domestic fuel, throughout that section of country. The first coal sent from Pittsburgh to an eastern market was shipped to Philadelphia in 1803. It was carried by the Louisiana, a boat of 350 tons burden, and was sold at the rate of thirty-seven and a half cents per bushel. From that time the increase in the mining of bituminous coal in the Pittsburgh region has been steady and enormous. Its presence, its quality and abundance, have induced the establishment of great manufacturing enterprises in that section of the State, and many millions of tons of it are sent every year to the markets of the seaboard.

Pennsylvania was a region much in favor with the North American Indians, and it is more than probable that they were aware, to some extent, of the existence of mineral wealth beneath her soil, long before white men ever came among them.

Besides the numerous outcroppings of coal which, in their journeyings, they must have crossed and recrossed for centuries, there were many places where the coal seams, having been cut through by creeks and rivers, were exposed fully to view. In this way, in the Wyoming district, the seven feet vein along the Nanticoke Creek had been disclosed, and the nine feet vein on Ransom's Creek at Plymouth; while at Pittston the Susquehanna River had bared the coal seams in the faces of its rocky banks, and up the Lackawanna the black strata were frequently visible. But whatever knowledge the Indians had on the subject was, with proverbial reticence, kept to themselves. It is said that about the year 1750 a party of Indians brought a bag of coal to a gunsmith living near Nazareth in Pennsylvania, but refused to say where they had obtained it. The gunsmith burned it successfully in the forge which he used for the purpose of repairing their guns.

The presumption that the Indians knew something of the uses of coal, and actually mined it, is borne out by the following incident: In the year 1766 a trader by the name of John Anderson was settled at Wyoming, and carried on a small business as a shopkeeper, trading largely with the red men. In September of that year a company of six Nanticoke, Conoy, and Mohican Indians visited the governor at Philadelphia, and made to him the following address: —

" Brother, — As we came down from Chenango

we stopped at Wyoming, where we had a mine in two places, and we discovered that some white people had been at work in the mine, and had filled three canoes with the ore; and we saw their tools with which they had dug it out of the ground, where they had made a hole at least forty feet long and five or six feet deep. It happened formerly that some white people did take, now and then, only a small bit and carry it away, but these people have been working at the mine, and have filled their canoes. We desire that you will tell us whether you know anything of this matter, or if it be done by your consent. We inform you that there is one John Anderson, a trader, now living at Wyoming, and we suspect that he, or somebody by him, has robbed our mine. This man has a store of goods there, and it may happen when the Indians see their mine robbed they will come and take away his goods."

There is little doubt that the mines referred to were coal mines. The presence of coal on the same side of the river a few miles below Wyoming was certainly known, if not at that time then very soon afterward; for in 1768 Charles Stewart made a survey of the Manor of Sunbury opposite Wilkes Barre for the "Proprietaries'" government, and on the original map of the survey "stone coal" is noted as appearing on the site of what is now called Rosshill.

This valley of Wyoming, the seat of such vast,

THE DISCOVERY OF COAL. 45

mineral wealth, was first settled by people from Connecticut in 1762, and in the fall of that year they reported the discovery of coal.

These energetic, enterprising Yankee settlers could not fail to know the location of the coal beds before they had been long in the valley. Some of them were probably familiar with the English bituminous coals, which were then being exported in small quantities to America under the name of "sea coal;" and from the fact that our anthracite was known to them as "stone coal" it is probable that there were those among them who knew that the English people had a very hard coal which they could not burn, and to which they had given the name "stone coal." Specimens of this Wyoming valley stone coal had already been gathered and sent to England for examination. Indeed, there is no doubt that the first anthracite coal ever found by white men in the United States was discovered in this valley. But these Yankee settlers could not make their stone coal burn. Repeated trials met with repeated failures. There was one among them, however, Obadiah Gore, a blacksmith, who would not be discouraged. In 1769 he took a quantity of these coals to the blacksmith's shop conducted by him and his brother, put them in his forge, and continued his efforts and experiments until finally the black lumps yielded to his persistency, and he had the satisfaction of seeing the blue flames dart from them, and the red color creep over them, and of feeling the intense heat sent out by their combustion. But their ignition and burning were dependent upon the strong air current sent through them by the bellows; without that he could do nothing with them.

So this Yankee blacksmith, who was afterwards one of the associate judges of the courts of Luzerne County, became, so far as is known, the first white man to demonstrate practically the value of anthracite coal as a fuel. The success of Gore's experiments soon became known, other smiths began to recognize the merits of the lately despised stone coal, and it was not long before the forge fires of nearly every smithy in the region were ablaze with anthracite.

The fame of the new fuel soon spread beyond the limits of the valley, and if the difficulties of transportation checked its use elsewhere, the knowledge of how to use it in forges and furnaces was not uncommon. The demand for it overcame, at times, even the obstacles in the way of shipment, and it was sent to points at long distances from the mines.

In 1776 the proprietary government of Pennsylvania had an armory at Carlisle in that State, in which they were manufacturing firearms to be used by the Continental troops in the war with Great Britain; and the first coal ever sent out from the Wyoming valley was shipped by them

THE DISCOVERY OF COAL 47

to Carlisle during that year and the succeeding years of the war, for use in their armory.

The next discoveries of anthracite were made in what is now know as the Southern coal field. It had long been a matter of tradition among the stolid German farmers of Pennsylvania that coal existed in the rugged hills along the Lehigh River, but no one succeeded in finding it there until the year 1791. It was then discovered by one Philip Ginther, a hunter and backwoodsman, who who had built a rough cabin in the forest near the Mauch Chunk mountain, and there gave to himself and his family a precarious support by killing game, large and small, carrying it to the nearest settlement, and exchanging it at the village store for the necessaries of life. Telling the story afterward, himself, he said that at one time the supply of food in his cabin chanced to run out, and he started into the woods with his gun in quest of something which should satisfy the hunger of those who were at home. It was a most unsuccessful hunting expedition. The morning passed, the afternoon went by, night approached, but his game-bag was still empty. He was tired, hungry, and sadly disappointed. A drizzling rain set in as he started homeward across the Mauch Chunk mountain, darkness was coming rapidly on, and despondency filled his mind as he thought of the expectant faces of little ones at home to whom he was returning empty-handed. Making his way slowly through the thick, wet undergrowth, and still looking about him, if perchance something in the way of game might yet come within the range of his gun, his foot happened to strike a hard substance which rolled away before him. He looked down at it, and then bent over and picked it up, and saw by the deepening twilight that it was black. He was familiar with the traditions of the country concerning the existence of stone coal in this region, and he began to wonder if this, indeed, was not a specimen of it. He carried the black lump home with him that night, and the next day he set out with it to find Colonel Jacob Weiss at Fort Allen, now Weissport, to whom he exhibited what he had found. Colonel Weiss became deeply interested in the matter, and brought the specimen to Philadelphia, where he submitted it to the inspection of John Nicholson, Michael Hillegas, and Charles Cist. These men, after assuring themselves that it was really anthracite coal, authorized Colonel Weiss to make such a contract with Ginther as would induce him to point out the exact spot where the mineral was found. It happened that the hunter coveted a vacant piece of land in the vicinity containing a fine water-power and mill-site, and on Colonel Weiss agreeing to obtain a patent for him from the State for the desired lot of land, he very readily gave all the information in his possession concerning the "stone coal."

In the Pottsville district of the Southern anthracite region coal was discovered at about the same time as in the Mauch Chunk field. This discovery too was made by accident, and the discoverer in this case also was a hunter, Nicholas Allen. He had been out with his gun all day, and at nightfall had found himself too far away from his home to make the attempt to reach it. He accordingly built a fire under a projecting ledge at the foot of Broad Mountain, and, lying down by it, soon fell asleep. He was wakened in the night by a strong light shining on his eyes, and by the sensation of great heat. Springing to his feet, he discovered that the ledge itself was burning, or, as he afterward expressed it, "that the mountain was on fire." He could not understand the phenomenon, and remained in the vicinity until morning, when he saw, by daylight, that what he had thought to be a ledge of rocks was really a projecting outcrop of mineral coal, which had become ignited from his camp-fire of sticks. Whether this story is or is not authentic, it is certain that no practical results attended the discovery of coal in this region. It was not until twenty-six years after Obadiah Gore's experiments in the Wyoming valley that coal was successfully burned here in a blacksmith's forge. The attempt was made by one Whetstone, and met with the same marked success that had attended the earlier effort. But owing to the difficulty still generally experienced in combustion, the coal of this region was not generally used until after the year 1806. In that year David Berlin, another blacksmith, experimented with it in his forge, with such complete success that a new impetus was given to the coal trade, mining was resumed, and the new fuel came into general use in the blacksmiths' shops of the vicinity.

In the Middle anthracite district coal was not discovered until 1826. This discovery also was made by a hunter, John Charles. On one of his hunting expeditions he chanced to find a groundhog's hole, and, laying down his rifle, he began to dig for his game. In the course of the excavation he uncovered a projecting shelf of stone coal. He made his discovery known, further explorations were set on foot, the coal bed was located, and a company called the Hazleton Coal Company was formed to work the field.

From these several points of discovery the search for anthracite coal was extended in all directions, the limits of the beds were eventually defined, and each field was surveyed and mapped with much care.

CHAPTER VI.

THE INTRODUCTION OF COAL INTO USE.

AT the beginning of the present century the anthracite or stone coal was in general use, in all the districts where it was found, as a fuel for the blacksmith's fire and the iron worker's forge. This, however, was the limit of its utility. It was thought to be necessary to force a strong artificial air current up through it to make it burn, and since this could not well be done in grates, stoves, or furnaces, there was no demand for coal for domestic use, or for the great manufacturing industries. Efforts were indeed made to overcome this difficulty. Schemes without number were set on foot and abandoned. It was proposed, at one time, to force air through a tube to the under part of the grate by means of clockwork operated by a weight or by a spring. But the cost of such an arrangement made it impracticable.

It seems, however, that Weiss, Cist, and Hillegas, who were developing the discovery made by Ginther in the Mauch Chunk mountain, also solved the problem of burning the stone coal without an artificial draft. They had sent specimens of their coals to Philadelphia, and presumably had accompanied them with instructions as to the proper method of burning them. This presumption is borne out by certain letters sent to Jacob Cist of Wilkes Barre, a son of Charles Cist the printer, who was in company with Weiss and Hillegas. Two of these letters are now in the possession of the Wyoming Historical and Geological Society at Wilkes Barre. An extract from one of them reads as follows: —

"I have experienced the use of them" (the Lehigh coals) "in a close stove and also in a fireplace that may be closed and opened at pleasure, so constructed, as to cause a brisk current of air to pass up through a small contracted grate on which they were laid. I find them more difficult to be kindled than the Virginia coal, yet a small quantity of dry wood laid on the grate under them is sufficient to ignite them, which being done, they continue to burn while a sufficient amount be added to keep up the combustion, occasionally stirring them to keep down the ashes. They produce no smoke, contain no sulphur, and when well ignited exhibit a vivid bright appearance, all which render them suitable for warming rooms."

This letter is dated "Philadelphia, Feb. 15th 1803," and is signed "Oliver Evans."

The second letter is similar in its recommendation and report of success, and states that the writer, "Fred^k Graff, clerk of the Water

INTRODUCTION OF COAL INTO USE. 53

Works of Phil[a] . . . made a trial of the Lehigh coals in the year 1802 in the large stove at the Pennsylvania Bank in Phil[a]."

So far as is known these are the first recorded instances of any successful attempts to burn anthracite coal in grates and stoves. Dr. James of Philadelphia has also left on record the fact that he made constant use of anthracite coal for heating purposes from the year 1804.

These well-authenticated instances of the use of anthracite appear to destroy the commonly accepted belief that Judge Jesse Fell of Wilkes Barre was the first person whose attempts to burn this coal in an open grate were rewarded with complete success. Nevertheless the value of Judge Fell's experiments cannot be questioned, nor can he be deprived of the full measure of credit due to him for bringing those experiments to a successful issue.

Until the year 1808 all efforts in the Wyoming valley to burn the "stone coal" of the region withwithout an artificial air blast had utterly failed. People did not believe that it could be done. The successes of Evans and Graff in this direction were either not known or not credited. It is certain that Judge Fell had not heard of them. His opinion that this coal could be made to burn in an open fireplace was based wholly on the reasoning of his own mind. He was a member of the Society of Friends, and had come to Wilkes

Barre some years before from Berks County. He was a blacksmith by trade, the proprietor of the best hotel in town, and he came afterward to be one of the associate judges of Luzerne County. When he had fully considered the matter of burning the stone coal, and had reached definite conclusions, he began to experiment. At first he constructed a grate of green hickory sticks, and the presumption is that the fire he kindled in it was a success; for he began, immediately afterward, to make an iron grate similar to the grates now in use. The work was done by his nephew Edward Fell and himself in the blacksmith shop of the former, and was completed in a single day. Judge Fell took the grate home late in the afternoon and set it with brick in the fireplace of his bar-room. In the evening he kindled in it, with oak wood, a glowing coal fire, and invited a large number of the most respected citizens of the place to come in and see the stone coal burn. Only a few came, however, in response to his invitation; they believed his theory to be impracticable, and feared that they might be made the victims of a hoax. But to those who came the fire was a revelation. It cleared the way for immense possibilities. Judge Fell himself realized the importance of his discovery, and thought the incident worthy of record. Being a devoted member of the order of Free and Accepted Masons, he chose from his library a book entitled " The Free Mason's Monitor," and wrote on the fly-leaf, in a clear, bold hand, this memorandum:—

"Fe'b 11th, of Masonry 5808. Made the experiment of burning the common stone coal of the valley in a grate in a common fire place in my house, and find it will answer the purpose of fuel; making a clearer and better fire, at less expense, than burning wood in the common way.

[Signed] JESSE FELL.

"BOROUGH OF WILKESBARRE,
  February 11th 1808."

The complete success of Judge Fell's experiment was soon noised abroad, and a new era of usefulness for anthracite coal set in. From Wilkes Barre up and down the entire Wyoming valley fireplaces for wood were discarded and grates were set for the burning of the new domestic fuel. This was followed, not long after, by the introduction of stoves, so that by 1820, says Stewart Pearce in his "Annals of Luzerne County," grates and coal stoves were in general use throughout the valley, coal for domestic purposes selling at three dollars per ton. At the time of Judge Fell's experiment there was no outside market for the product of the mines of the Wyoming valley. The distances to the large cities and manufacturing centres were too great, the means of transportation too rude, and the knowledge of the use of anthracite too limited, to warrant any serious effort to create a foreign market for it. The attempt had nevertheless been made in 1807 by Abijah Smith, who shipped an ark-load of coal down the Susquehanna River to Columbia, and was obliged to leave it there unsold.

In 1808 the experiment was repeated by Abijah and his brother John, who, profiting by the success of Judge Fell's late experiment, took with them an iron grate, set it up at Columbia, and proceeded to demonstrate to the doubting inhabitants the practical value of their coal as a domestic fuel. The venture proved successful, and after this they found no difficulty in selling at the river towns all the coal they could mine. After 1812 they extended their trade by running their coal to Havre de Grace, and sending it thence by schooner to New York.

The success which attended the efforts of the Smiths appears to have been an inducement to other enterprising citizens of the Wyoming valley to embark in the coal trade, and in 1813 and 1814 Colonel George M. Hollenback, Colonel Lord Butler, Joseph Wright, Esq., and Crandal Wilcox all engaged in the mining and shipping of coal. They sent the product of the mines down the river in arks, and up to 1830 85,000 tons had been mined in the valley for such shipment. After that year coal was sent by the North Branch Canal just completed to Nanticoke, and in 1846 the Lehigh and Susquehanna Railroad pierced the valley, and opened a new era in

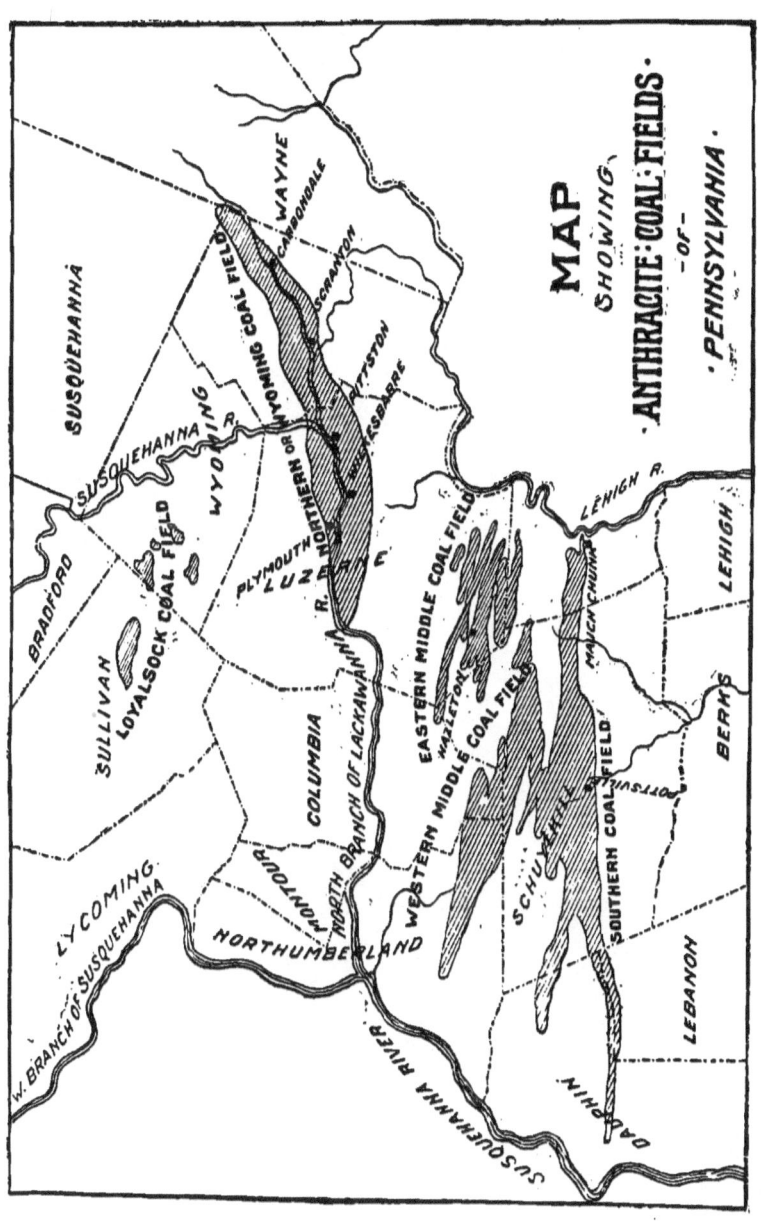

INTRODUCTION OF COAL INTO USE. 57

transportation. So it came about that this region, which in 1807 opened the anthracite coal trade with a shipment of fifty-five tons, sent to market in 1887 a grand total of 19,684,929 tons.

In the mean time Weiss, Cist, and Hillegas pushed their coal enterprise on the Mauch Chunk mountain, opening what was afterward known as the Great Summit Mine, and in 1803 started six ark-loads of coal down the Lehigh River, to be floated to its junction with the Delaware, and thence to Philadelphia. Only two of the arks reached their destination, the others having met with disaster on the way, owing to swift currents and unskillful navigation. Of the two cargoes that arrived safely at Philadelphia not a lump could be sold. The owners made strenuous efforts to find a market for it, but people did not wish to purchase a fuel that they could not make burn. At last the city authorities were appealed to, and, after some hesitation, they agreed to take the coal and try to make use of it for a steam-engine employed at the city waterworks. This they did; but all their attempts to make the alleged fuel burn proved unavailing. They finally gave up the task in disgust, declared the coal to be a nuisance, and caused what remained of it to be broken up and spread on the footpaths of the public grounds, in place of gravel. This was indeed a most ignominious failure. It caused a sudden cessation of mining operations at Summit

Hill, and for several years the Lehigh Mine Company, utterly discouraged, made no effort to retrieve its fallen fortunes. William Turnbull attempted to revive the project a few years later, but his effort also met with a dismal failure.

In 1813 Charles Miner, Jacob Cist, and John W. Robinson, all of Wilkes Barre, renewed the enterprise at Summit Hill with great energy, and on the 9th of August, 1814, started their first ark-load of coal down the river to Philadelphia. Before it had gone eighty rods from the place of starting it struck a ledge which tore a hole in the bow of the boat, "and," Mr. Miner says, "the lads stripped themselves nearly naked to stop the rush of water with their clothes." After many and varied adventures on the swift currents of the rivers the ark reached its destination on the following Sunday morning at eight o'clock, having been five days on the way. Its arrival had been anticipated by its owners, and they had called public attention to its cargo by means of handbills printed in both English and German, and distributed freely throughout the city. These handbills, besides advertising the coal, gave information as to the method of burning it in grates, stoves, and smith's forges. They were also accompanied by printed certificates from blacksmiths and others attesting the value and availability of the Lehigh coal as a fuel. The owners of the ark went still farther. They put up stoves in conspicuous public

INTRODUCTION OF COAL INTO USE. 59

places in the city, built coal fires in them, and invited the people to stop and inspect them. They went to private houses and prevailed on the inmates to be allowed to kindle anthracite fires in the grates which had been built for the use of Liverpool coals. They attended at blacksmith's shops, and even bribed the journeymen to give their coals a fair trial in the forge. Thus, by persistent and industrious, nay by presumptuous, efforts, these men succeeded in awakening public interest in their enterprise, and in creating a demand for their wares. The proprietors of the Lehigh coals gave particular attention also to the instruction of the people in the matter of igniting the new fuel. Having once disabused them of the idea that a strong artificial air current was necessary, the next step was to prevent them from disturbing the coals constantly by poking, punching, and raking them, a proceeding which the uninitiated seemed to consider of prime importance, in order to induce them to ignite. And, strange as it may seem, this fallacy was the hardest to overcome. Among the purchasers of the Lehigh coals in 1814 was the firm of White & Hazard, manufacturers of iron wire at the falls of the Schuylkill. They had been told by Mr. Joshua Malin, proprietor of a rolling mill, that he had succeeded in using the new fuel, and as the Virginia coal was very scarce at that time, White & Hazard decided to test the qualities of the anthracite.

They purchased a cart-load of it, paying a dollar a bushel for it, and took it to their works. Here they tried to build a fire with it in their furnace, giving it what they considered the most skillful manipulation and the most assiduous attention. Their efforts were in vain. The entire cart-load was wasted in a futile attempt to make the coals burn. Nothing daunted, they obtained another cartload, and determined to spend the night, if need should be, in the work of building a coal fire. And they did spend the night. But when morning came they were apparently as far from the attainment of their object as ever. They had poked and punched and raked; they had labored incessantly; but notwithstanding the most constant manipulation, the coals above the burning wood would not sufficiently ignite. By this time the men were disheartened and disgusted, and slamming the door of the furnace, they left the mill in despair, and went to breakfast. It happened that one of them had left his jacket in the furnace room, and returning for it about half an hour later, he discovered that the furnace door was red-hot. In great surprise he flung the door open and found the interior glowing with intense white heat. The other hands were immediately summoned, and four separate parcels of iron were heated and rolled by the same fire before it required renewing. Seeking for the cause of this unexpected result the men came to the conclusion that it was due to simply letting the fire alone, a theory the correctness of which they afterward abundantly proved. Thus, by chance, these men hit upon the secret of success in the matter of building a fire of anthracite coals. That secret is simply to throw the coals loosely on the burning wood, and then *let them alone*. The incident at White & Hazard's mills becoming generally known, people learned more from it about the process of building a coal fire than they had learned from all their previous instruction.

Nevertheless the enterprise of the Lehigh operators was still not destined to meet with success. They had embarked in the coal trade in 1814, while the war with Great Britain was still in progress, when it was impossible to procure coal from England, and when coal from the Richmond district was very scarce. They were therefore able to obtain fourteen dollars per ton for the Lehigh coal, but even at this price the cost and risk of mining and shipping was so great that the business was barely a paying one. In 1815, however, peace was concluded with Great Britain, the market was again opened to the reception of foreign coals, and the Lehigh operators, being unable to compete with the sellers of soft coal, were obliged to abandon the field.

Notwithstanding the efforts and energy of these proprietors the Summit Hill mining industry did not pay, and in 1817 the mines passed into the hands of Josiah White and Erskine Hazard. They perfected a system of slack-water navigation on the Lehigh, and in 1820 made their first shipment of 365 tons. The tables commonly printed showing the growth of the anthracite coal trade usually make that trade begin with this shipment of Lehigh coal in 1820. This, however, is not quite correct, as we have seen that coal was sent to market from the Wyoming region at a much earlier date. It is remarkable that, whereas in 1820 the 365 tons of Lehigh coal stocked the market, in 1831, the year in which the system of slack water navigation was superseded by shipment on the Delaware division of the Pennsylvania Canal, this region sent down 40,966 tons. And in 1887 there was sent to market from the Lehigh district a total of 4,347,061 tons, an amount which would have been much greater had not a prolonged strike of coal miners seriously interfered with the output.

In the Schuylkill region of the Southern coal field similar obstacles to the introduction of coal were encountered. Nicholas Allen, the discoverer of coal in that region, had formed a partnership with Colonel George Shoemaker, and the firm had purchased a tract of coal land near Pottsville, on which they began mining operations in the year 1812. They raised several wagon loads of coal, and offered it for sale in the vicinity, but with the exception of a few blacksmiths, who had been taught its value as a fuel by Colonel Shoemaker, no one could be found to purchase it. Allen soon became disheartened and sold his entire interest in the property to his partner, who, still persisting in the enterprise, mined a considerable quantity of the coal, filled ten wagons with it, and took it to Philadelphia in quest of a market. But it did not meet with a ready sale. People looked at the coals curiously, considered them to be nothing more than black stones, and, seeing no reason why they should burn better than stones of any other color, would not buy them.

Colonel Shoemaker sounded the praises of his wares so vigorously and persistently, however, that at last a few purchasers were induced to take them in small quantities, just for trial. The trials, as usual, proved to be unsuccessful, and the people who had purchased the coals, believing they had been victimized, denounced Colonel Shoemaker as a cheat and a swindler; while one person, whose wrath rose to a high pitch, procured a warrant for the colonel's arrest, on the charge that he was a common impostor. At this stage of the proceedings, Colonel Shoemaker, believing discretion to be the better part of valor, quietly left the city and started toward his home by a circuitous route, driving, it is said, some thirty miles out of his way, in order to avoid the officer of the law holding the warrant for his arrest.

This was indeed a discouraging beginning for

the Schuylkill coal trade. Fortunately, however, not all of the colonel's customers at Philadelphia had met with failure in the effort to burn his coal. Messrs. Mellen & Bishop, a firm of iron factors in Delaware County, at the earnest solicitation of Colonel Shoemaker, made the experiment with the small quantity of coals purchased by them, and finding that the fuel burned successfully they announced that fact through the Philadelphia newspapers. Other iron workers were thus induced to try the coal, and finally all the furnaces along the Schuylkill had open doors for it. Eventually it came into use for the purpose of generating steam, the experiments of John Price Wetherill in that direction having been only partially satisfactory, but those at the Phœnixville iron works in 1825 meeting with complete success.

Still the prices which coal commanded in the Philadelphia market were not sufficient to pay for the labor of mining it and the cost of shipping it. So that, prior to 1818, nearly all the coal mined in the Schuylkill region was sold to the blacksmiths of the surrounding country. In that year, however, the improvements of the Schuylkill navigation were completed, and afforded an additional, though not by any means safe or sufficient, outlet for the products of the mines. By 1826 and 1827 the growing importance of the coal trade became manifest, the Schuylkill navigation system was placed in excellent repair, and the mining business of the district grew rapidly to enormous proportions.

The northeasterly extension of the Wyoming coal basin, leaving the Susquehanna River at Pittston, follows the valley of the Lackawanna up to a point seven miles beyond Carbondale, where it cuts slightly into the counties of Wayne and Susquehanna, and there runs out. This extension is known as the Lackawanna region. Coal was dug up and experimented with here at the beginning of the present century. Its outcrop at the river bank was noted by Preston, a surveyor, in 1804. In 1812 it was mined at Providence and burned in a rude grate by H. C. L. Von Storch. About this time the brothers William and Maurice Wurts, having been attracted by the mineral wealth of the region, came there from Philadelphia and began explorations for the purpose of ascertaining the location, area, and quality of the beds of anthracite coal. William, the younger brother, in the course of his wanderings through the rugged hills and thick forests of the country, chanced to meet a hunter by the name of David Nobles, who, having fled from the adjoining county of Wayne to avoid imprisonment for debt, was leading a precarious existence in the woods. Nobles was well acquainted with the country, knew where the outcroppings of coal were, and having entered into the service of Wurts, rendered him most valuable assistance.

Their investigations having proved the presence of large bodies of coal, the Wurts brothers next procured title to the lands containing it, and then turned their attention to the problem of finding an outlet to market. They decided finally to ship coal on rafts by the Wallenpaupack Creek to the Lackawaxen, by the Lackawaxen to the Delaware, and thence to Philadelphia. This method was experimented on from 1814 to 1822 with varying degrees of disaster. In the year last mentioned they succeeded in taking to Philadelphia 100 tons of coal, only to find the market flooded with 2,240 tons of Lehigh coal. Competition was apparently hopeless; but instead of abandoning the enterprise, as men of less energy and perseverance would now have done, Maurice Wurts turned his attention to a new project. This was nothing less than to make an outlet to the New York market by building a canal which should reach from the Hudson River at Rondout, across to the Delaware at Port Jervis, and thence up that stream and the Lackawaxen to the nearest practicable point east of the coal beds. But when that point should be reached there would still be the Moosic Mountain, with its towering heights and precipitous bluffs, lying between the boats and the mines. The Wurts brothers did not acknowledge this to be a serious obstacle. They proposed to overcome this difficulty by building across the mountains a railroad, which should consist largely of inclined planes, the cars to be drawn up and let down these planes by means of stationary steam-engines, and to move along the stretches between the planes by force of gravity. Having formed their plans they set to work to carry them out. They procured the necessary legislation from the States of New York and Pennsylvania, they secured a charter in 1823-25 for a corporation known as the Delaware and Hudson Canal Company, and by dint of supreme personal effort they succeeded in obtaining capital enough to begin and carry on the work. In 1828 the canal was completed to its terminus at Honesdale, the gravity railroad having been already constructed from the coal fields to that point, and in 1829 the company began to ship coal to tide-water on the Hudson. It was a bold and ingenious scheme, and for those days it was an enterprise of immense proportions. That these two men conceived it and carried it out in the face of great difficulties and against overwhelming odds entitles them to a place in those higher orders of genius that are touched with the light of the heroic. The Lackawanna region has been pierced by many other lines of railway, and to-day by these great highways a vast amount of Lackawanna coal is sent to the eastern cities and the seaboard.

But as a rule, men who invested their money in coal lands in the early days after the discovery of coal lost the amount of the investment. They, with prophetic vision, saw the comfort, the commerce, the manufactures, of a nation dependent on the products of the coal mines, but the people at large could not see so far. These pioneers made ready to supply an anticipated demand, but it did not come. Talking did not bring it. Exhibitions of the wonderful utility of the black coals served to arouse but a passing interest. No other product of the globe which has obtained a position of equal importance ever had to fight its way into public favor with such persistent effort through so many years. But when at last its worth became generally recognized, when the people had reached the conclusion that they wanted it, and its value in dollars had become fixed and permanent, then the pioneers of the industry had vanished from the field; they were disheartened, destitute, or dead; new hands and brains took up the work, matured the plans of the elders, and reaped the fortunes of which former generations had sown the seed.

In the beginning the coal lands were mostly divided into small tracts, and held by persons many of whom thought to open mines on their property and carry on the business of mining as an individual enterprise. This plan of work was partially successful so long as coal could be dug from the outcrop and carted away like stones from a quarry; but when it became necessary, as it soon did, to penetrate more deeply into the earth for the article of trade, then the cost of shafting, tunneling, and mining in general usually exceeded the resources of the individual operator, and either he succumbed to financial distress, or disposed of his mining interests to men or firms with more money. As the art of mining advanced with its necessities, it was learned, sometimes after bitter experience, that the business was profitable only when a large amount of capital was behind it. Therefore men who had invested a few thousand dollars transferred their interests to men who had a few hundred thousand to invest, and these, in turn, associating other capitalists with them, doubled or trebled the investment or ran it into the millions, forming companies or corporations to accomplish with their more perfect organization that which would be impossible to the individual. So it has come about that in these later days the individual operators have given place largely to the corporations; those who still remain in the field often operating their mines on a small capital at great disadvantage. In the bituminous regions, however, this rule does not hold good. There the coal lies near the surface, is accessible, and easily mined. It needs only to be carried to the river bank and screened as it is loaded into boats and started on its way to market. Compared with the anthracite regions, it requires but a small capital here to sustain an extensive plant, and produce a large quantity of coal. Therefore we find, as we should expect to find, that in the bituminous districts the bulk of the coal is produced by individuals, firms, and small companies. In the anthracite regions, however, this rule is reversed. Of the 36,204,000 tons of anthracite produced in the year 1887, 16,109,387 tons, or nearly one half, were mined by five great companies; namely: The Philadelphia and Reading; Delaware and Hudson; Delaware, Lackawanna, and Western; Lehigh Valley; and Pennsylvania Coal Company. The immense out-put of as many more large corporations left but a very small proportion of the total product to the small companies, firms, and individuals.

It follows, as a matter of course, that the acreage of coal lands held by these companies bears the same proportion to the total acreage that their coal out-put bears to the entire coal out-put. That is, they either own or hold under lease the great bulk of the coal beds of the anthracite regions. The value of coal lands varies with the number, thickness, and accessibility of the coal seams contained in it. In the very early days of anthracite mining these lands were purchased from farmers and others at from twenty and thirty dollars to one hundred dollars per acre. Before 1850 the price had advanced, in the Wyoming region, to from seventy-five dollars to two hundred dollars per acre. Recently a piece of coal land was sold in this region for $1,200 per acre, and another piece, containing thirty-six acres, was sold at the rate of $1,500 per acre. Perhaps from

INTRODUCTION OF COAL INTO USE. 71

$800 to $1,000 per acre might be considered an average price. In the Middle and Southern anthracite regions the coal lands are of still greater value ; not because the quality of the mineral is better, nor because the market for it is more accessible, but because the coal seams dip at a greater angle, and, therefore, a given number of acres contains a larger amount of coal.

The system of leasing coal lands to coal operators is a very common one, especially in the Wyoming valley, where the surface is so richly adapted to agricultural uses. The proprietor can, in this way, retain the use of the soil, and at the same time reap a handsome profit from the development of the mineral deposits beneath it. He invests no capital, runs no risk, and is sure of a steady income. As it is usual to work leased coal seams, wherever convenient, from openings made on the adjoining lands owned by the company, it is not often that the surface of leased property is interfered with, or if it is, but a comparatively small area of it is taken. The contract of lease usually stipulates that a certain royalty shall be paid to the lessor for each ton of coal mined, and it binds the lessee to mine not less than a certain number of tons each year ; or at least to pay royalties on not less than a certain number of tons each year, whether that number is or is not mined. Twenty years or more ago coal lands in the Wyoming district could be leased at the rate of ten cents per ton. Lately a large body of coal land was rented to the Lehigh Valley Coal Company at forty-five cents per ton, and it is said that one proprietor at Kingston has been offered a lease at fifty cents per ton, and has refused it. Perhaps from twenty-five cents to thirty-five cents per ton would be an average rate.

As an example of the immense purchases made by these companies, it may be noted that the Philadelphia and Reading Company, in 1871, purchased one hundred thousand acres of coal lands in the Schuylkill region, at a cost of forty millions of dollars. And as an example of the amount of business done in a year, it may be noted that the Delaware and Hudson Canal Company paid in 1887 $5,019,147.16 for the single item of mining coal, and that their coal sales for the same year amounted to $10,100,118.69.

This concentration of coal lands and coal mining in the hands of great corporations, aside from its tendency to stifle healthy competition, is productive of many benefits. Coal can be mined much cheaper when the mining is done on a large scale. This is the rule, indeed, in all productive industries. An enterprise backed by the combined capital of many individuals is more certain to become successful and permanent than an enterprise inaugurated by, and carried on with, the entire capital of a single individual. Especially is this the rule in a business attended with as

INTRODUCTION OF COAL INTO USE. 73

much risk as is the business of coal mining. One person may put his entire fortune of two or three hundred thousand dollars into a single colliery. A depression in the coal trade, a strike among the miners, an explosion, or a fire would be very apt to bring financial ruin on him. A company, with its great resources and its elastic character, can meet and recover from an adverse incident of this kind with scarcely a perceptible shock to its business. It is simply one of the items of loss which it is prepared to cover with a larger item of profit. There is also the additional assurance that all work that is done will be well done. The most careful observations and calculations are made of the amount and quality of included coal in any tract of land before it is purchased, and the best surveyors are employed to mark out the boundary lines of lands. The services of the most skillful mining engineers are retained, at salaries which no individual operator could afford to pay. Their forces are well organized, their mining operations are conducted with system and economy, and they are able to keep abreast of the age in all inventions and appliances that insure greater facility in mining and manufacturing, and greater safety to the workmen. Their employees are paid promptly at stated periods, and the possibility of a workman losing his wages by reason of neglect or failure on the part of his employer is reduced to a minimum.

In general, it may be said that the control of the anthracite coal business by the great corporations, rather than by individual operators, is an undoubted benefit, not only to all the parties in direct interest, but to commerce and society as a whole. The only danger to be feared is from an abuse of the great powers to which these companies have attained; a danger which, thus far, has not seriously menaced the community.

CHAPTER VII.

THE WAY INTO THE MINES.

A WISE coal operator never begins to open a mine for the purpose of taking out coal until he knows the character of the bed and the quality of the mineral. This knowledge can only be obtained by an exhaustive search for, and a careful examination of, all surface indications, and by drilling or boring holes down to and through the strata of coal. This is called "prospecting." The examiner in a new field will first look for outcrops. He will follow up the valleys and inspect the ledges and the banks of streams. If he be so fortunate as to find an exposure of the coal seams, or of any one of them, he will measure its thickness, will calculate its dip and strike, and will follow its outcrop. He will also study and make careful note of the rock strata with which it is associated, for by this means he may be able to determine the probability of other seams lying above or below it. This examination of the rock strata he will make, whether coal is visible or not visible. It will be of much service to him. For instance, it is known that the great Baltimore vein in the Wyoming valley is usually overlaid by a coarse red sandstone. If the examiner finds rock of this character in that section, he has good reason to hope that coal lies beneath it. Under the lowest coal seam of the anthracite beds there is found, as a rule, a rock known as the conglomerate. If, therefore, the explorer finds an outcrop of conglomerate, he will know that, as a rule, he need not look for coal beyond it. This rock, coming to the surface on the westerly side of the Moosic range of mountains, marks the limit of the Lackawanna coal field toward the east. No one, having once studied the conglomerate rock, could mistake it for any other, though its composition is very simple. It is nothing more than white, water-worn quartz pebbles, held together by a firm, lead-colored cement. But it is a rock of unusual hardness and durability. It is proof against the erosive action of water, grows harder by exposure to the air, and has a consistency that approximates to that of iron. In the coal districts it is used largely for building purposes, where heavy walls and foundations are required. Experience has taught that there are no coal seams below the conglomerate, so that wherever this is found as a surface rock, or wherever it is pierced by the drill, it is usually unnecessary to explore below it. If no coal outcrop is found, the bed of a stream is searched for fragments of the mineral, and, if any are discovered, they are traced to their source. Coal is sometimes exposed where a tree has been uprooted by the wind, and pieces of it have been found in the soil thrown out at a groundhog's burrow.

Wagon roads crossing the country may be scanned for traces of the "smut" or "blossom." This is the decomposed outcrop, which has become mingled with the soil, and may be more readily distinguished in the bed of a traveled road than elsewhere. Other surface indications failing, the topographical features of this section of country should be studied. Wherever the coal seams come to the surface, being softer than the rock strata above and below them, they are disintegrated and eroded more rapidly by the action of the atmosphere and the elements. This wearing away of the exposed coal leaves the surface outline in the form of a bench or terrace, which follows the line of the outcrop. And this form is retained even with a thick deposit of soil over the edges of the strata. Small shafts may be sunk or tunnels driven through this thickness of earth, and the outcrop explored in this way. This process of examination is of more value in the bituminous than in the anthracite regions, since the bituminous coal, being soft, is more rapidly eroded, and the terrace formation resulting from such erosion is more distinct and certain. In these days, in the anthracite coal fields, there is hardly an area of any great extent in which mines have not been actually opened. These mines, therefore, in the facilities they afford for studying exposed strata and developed coal seams, offer the best means of acquiring knowledge concerning the coal beds of adjoining tracts. In a country where no surface indications of coal are found over a large area, it is hardly worth while to explore for it by boring. In the anthracite regions of Pennsylvania the limits of the coal beds are now so accurately defined that it is seldom necessary to bore for the purpose of testing the presence of coal. But it is always advisable, before opening a mine in a new field, to test the depth, dip, and quality of the coal and the character of the seams by sinking one or more bore holes. Surface measurements of a seam are, at best, very uncertain, as indications of its continuing character. The angle of dip may change radically before a depth of one hundred feet shall be reached. And coal undergoes so great deterioration by long exposure to the atmosphere that, in order to judge the quality of a coal bed, it is necessary to have a specimen fragment from it that has been hidden away in the rocks. Hence the necessity of boring.

Hand drills were generally used in the early days of prospecting, and a sand pump drew out the sludge or borings for examination. This was superseded by the spring pole method, which in turn gave way to the rope method in use in the oil regions, the borings in each case being carefully preserved for inspection. The diamond drill is the one now in common use in the coal regions. Its cutting end is in the form of a circle set with black, amorphous diamonds. It cuts an annular groove in the rock as it descends, forming a core, which is withdrawn with the drill, and which may be examined in vertical section. The sludge is washed out by a stream of water which passes down through the centre of the drill rod, and is forced back to the surface between the rod and the face of the bore hole. The invention of this rotary cutting drill is due to Leschot of Geneva, and the method of flushing the hole to Flauvelle.

After having obtained all possible information concerning his coal property, and, if he be wise, embodying it in the form of maps, the coal operator must decide where he shall make an opening for mining purposes, and what kind of an opening he shall make. The answers to these two questions are, to a certain extent, dependent on each other, as certain kinds of openings must be located at certain places. When coal was first gathered for experiment or observation, it was taken up loosely from the ground, where it had fallen or been broken down from the outcrop of some seam. As it came into demand for practical purposes, it was quarried from this outcrop backward and downward, as stones for building purposes are now quarried, the seam being uncovered as the work proceeded. This process was followed along the line of the outcrop, but excavations were not made to any considerable depth, owing to the great expense of uncovering the coal.

The open quarry system of mining coal has been successfully practiced in America in but a few places. One of these was the great Summit Hill open mine, near Mauch Chunk, where the Lehigh coal was first discovered. Here, on a hill-top, was a horizontal coal bed, some sixty acres in extent, and varying in thickness from fifteen to fifty feet. Over this was a covering of rock, slate, and earth from three to fifteen feet in thickness. This bed was mined by simply removing the covering and taking the coal out as from a quarry. Other examples of this method are seen at Hollywood Colliery, and at Hazleton No. 6 Colliery, both near Hazleton, in Luzerne County. There are isolated instances of this method of stripping elsewhere in the anthracite regions, but as a rule the conditions are not favorable for it. Ordinarily there are four methods of making an entrance into a mine for the purpose of taking out coal. These are known as the drift, the tunnel, the slope, and the shaft.

To the early miners the drift was the favorite mode of entry. Finding an exposed seam of coal in the face of a ledge or cliff, they would dig in on it and bring the coal out from the opening in wheelbarrows. A place was selected, if possible,

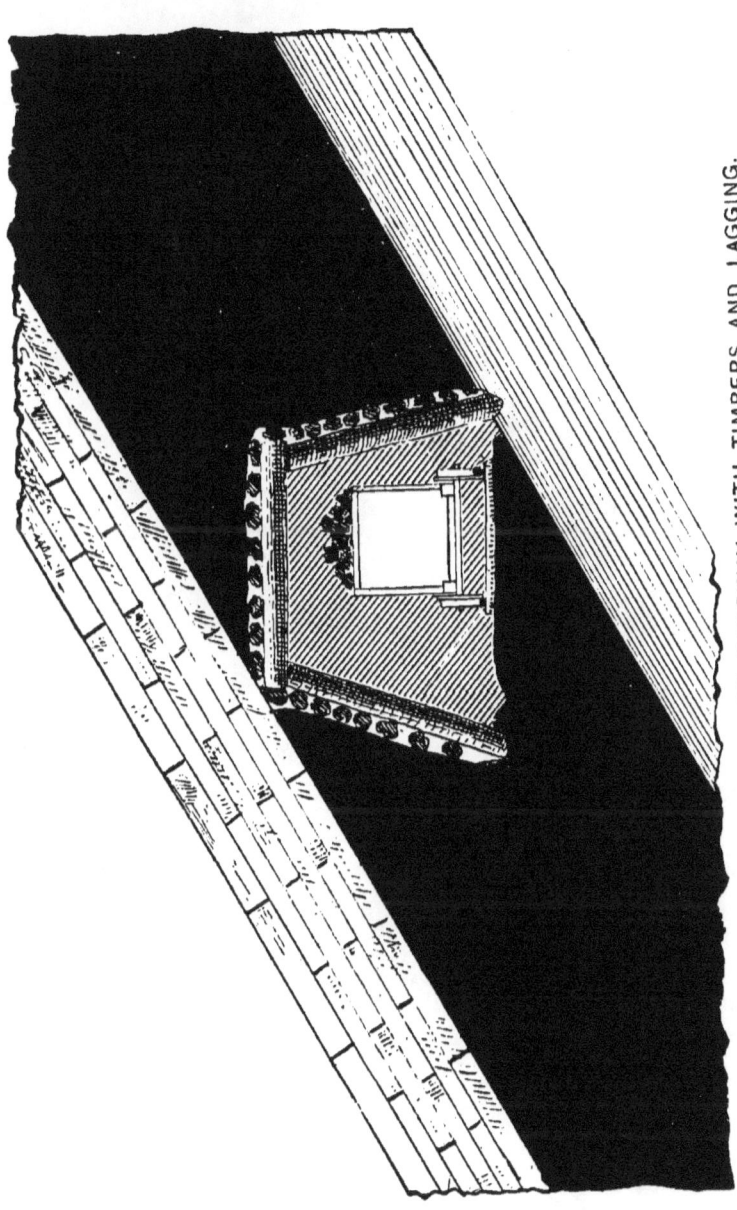

CROSS SECTION OF DRIFT OR GANGWAY WITH TIMBERS AND LAGGING.

where a creek or river ran at the base of the ledge, and the coal was dumped from the wheelbarrow directly into a boat. In default of a water way a wagon road was built at the foot of the hill or cliff, a platform extended out over it, and the coal was thus loaded from the wheelbarrow into the wagon.

The modern drift, though fashioned on an improved plan, is the simplest and least expensive way of making an entrance into a coal mine. The outline of the proposed opening is first marked out on the edge of the exposed coal seam. From fifteen to eighteen feet is an ordinary width to accommodate two tracks, and ten feet will readily accommodate one. Seven feet is an average height, though, if the seam be comparatively flat, the coal will be taken down until the rock is reached, even though a greater height should be attained. With this width and height the opening is cut into the hill through the coal seam. The floor of the drift must have a constant upward grade as it progresses inward, in order that the water may run out, and that loaded cars may be hauled more easily. The mouth of the drift must be above the level of the adjacent valley or stream, so that the water may be carried away, and the drift is therefore what is known as a water-level opening. It is usually necessary to support the roof and sides of the drift by timbers joined together in the form of a bent, and placed more or less closely to each other. These timbers are also sometimes lined by sticks placed behind and over them horizontally, and known as "lagging." It will be seen that the conditions under which the opening by drift may be made place a serious limitation on the use of this method. It will also now be seen why the drift is the simplest and most economical mode of making an entrance to a mine. In this method there is no expense for removing earth or for cutting through rock, nor any cost at any time of pumping water or of hoisting coal. When the fact is remembered that it sometimes costs from $50,000 to $100,000 to sink a deep shaft through hard rock, and that to this amount must be added the cost of buildings, machinery, and repairs, and the perpetual cost of pumping water and of hoisting coal, the economy of the drift method will be appreciated. But the day of drift mining in the anthracite regions has gone by. Those portions of the coal beds lying above water level have been largely mined out, and the areas of coal that are now accessible by drift are very limited. In the bituminous districts, however, where the seams lie comparatively flat and the coal is mostly above water level, the method by drift is still almost universally used.

Next to a drift, the tunnel is the simplest and most economical method, under certain circumstances, of making an entrance into a mine. This is a passage driven across the measures, and at right angles to the seam, in order to reach coal which at the point of opening is not exposed. The tunnel is usually driven into the side of a hill. The earth is first dug away until the rock is exposed, or, if the soil be too deep for that, only enough of it is taken to make a vertical face for the mouth of the tunnel. The opening is then driven into the hill at about the same width and height that a drift would be made, and in practically the same manner. If there is a section of earth tunneling at the mouth, the timbering must be close, and the lagging will be of heavy planks. When the solid rock is reached, however, it is not often that any timbering is necessary, the sides and roof being so hard and firm as not to need support. This passage is driven against the face of a coal seam, and when the coal is finally reached the tunnel proper ends, a passage is opened to the right and one to the left along the strike of the seam, and from these gangways the coal is mined. The tunnel, like the drift, must be above water level, and its floor must have a descending grade toward the mouth, to carry off water. The expense of the tunnel, and its superiority to the slope or shaft, will depend upon the distance through which the rock must be pierced before coal is reached. It is especially advisable, therefore, before opening a tunnel, to have an accurate map of the location and dip of the coal seams to be struck by it, otherwise no approximate calculation can be made of the extent or cost of the work.

In the anthracite districts, where the seams are sharply pitching, tunnels are driven in the interior of a mine from the workings of a seam already opened across the intervening measures to strike an adjacent seam. In this way two, three, or more coal seams can be worked, and the coal can all be brought out at one surface opening. This is virtually the only kind of tunneling that is now done in the anthracite regions; for, as has already been explained, the coal that lay above water level and was thus accessible by tunnel has now been mostly mined out.

If there is an outcrop of coal on the tract to be mined, and the dip of the seam is more than twenty degrees, it is usually advisable to enter the mine by means of a slope. This is a passage which, beginning at the outcrop, follows the coal seam down until the necessary depth is reached. It is driven in the coal. The distinction between the drift and the slope is that the drift is driven from the surface on the strike of the seam while the slope is driven on its dip. Where the coal seam comes within a moderate distance of the surface, as at an anticlinal ridge, a slope may be driven through the rock until the coal is reached at the axis, and from that point follow the seam down. Sometimes a shaft is sunk to the top of an anticlinal ridge, and from its foot two slopes are

driven, one down each side of the roll, in opposite directions. If the seam is very irregular, or if it is much broken by faults, there may be a great deal of rock cutting to be done in order to preserve the uniformity of grade necessary for the slope. The cost may, indeed, in this case, amount to more than would have been sufficient to sink a shaft to the same depth, although, as a rule, the entrance by slope should cost only about one fourth of that by shaft.

The same methods are employed in sinking a slope as are used in driving a drift, except that generally the timbering need not be so heavy. The minimum height of the slope is about $6\frac{1}{2}$ feet, the width at the top, or collar, about 8 feet, and the width at the bottom, or spread, about 12 feet. If a double track is desired the spread should be 18 feet and the collar 14 feet. In the Wyoming region, where the dip is usually less than twenty degrees, with infrequent outcrops, the slope is not in general use; but in the Southern coal field, where the dip varies from twenty degrees to the vertical, the slope is the most common method of entering a mine. There the opening is driven down for a distance of 300 feet, at which point gangways are started out to right and left, along the strike, and chambers driven from them back toward the surface. This is called the first lift. The slope is then continued downward for another distance of 300 feet, new gangways and chambers are laid off, and this is called the second lift. This process is continued until the synclinal basin is reached.

Where the dip of the slope is less than thirty degrees the coal is brought to the surface in the car into which it was first loaded in the mine. At a greater angle than this the ordinary mine car is superseded by a car or carriage especially adapted to carrying coal up a steep incline.

Where there is no outcrop in the tract to be mined, and the coal lies below water level, the best mode of making an entrance to it is by shaft. In the Wyoming region, since the upper veins have been so generally mined out, nearly all the openings are by shaft. The location of the shaft at the surface should be such that when it is completed its foot shall be at the bottom, or nearly at the bottom, of the synclinal valley into which it is sunk. As will be more readily seen hereafter, this is necessary in order to carry the water of the mine to the foot of the shaft, to facilitate the transportation of coal under ground, and to get room to open up the greatest possible working area. The depth to which a shaft must be sunk depends on the seam to be reached, and on the district in which it is located. At Carbondale, in the northeasterly extremity of the Wyoming basin, the average depth to the conglomerate or bed of the lowest coal seam is 250 feet. From Scranton to Pittston it is from 500 to 600 feet. At Wilkes Barre it is 1,200 feet. It reaches its greatest average depth a mile northeast of Nanticoke, where it is from 1,500 to 1,600 feet.

This will be the limit of depth for shafts in the Wyoming region. At present the average depth is from 300 to 400 feet, and there are few that are more than 800 feet deep. The red-ash vein to which most of the shafts are now being sunk is, at Pittston in the middle of the general basin, from 450 to 650 feet below the surface. In the southern anthracite region the average depth of shafts is somewhat greater, the maximum depth being reached in the vicinity of Pottsville, where the Pottsville deep shafts are about 1,600 feet in depth.

In beginning to open a shaft a rectangular space is staked out on the ground from four to eight feet wider and longer than the proposed dimensions of the shaft; and the soil and loose stones are thrown out from this larger area until bed rock is reached, which is usually done, except in the river bottom lands, within a depth of twenty feet.

From this rock as a foundation a cribbing of solid timber, twelve inches square, is built up to the surface on the four sides of the opening to prevent the earth from caving in. Sometimes heavy walls of masonry are built up instead of the timber cribbing, and though the original cost is greater, the purpose is far better answered by the stone curbing. When this has been completed, sinking through the rock goes on by the ordinary process of blasting, plumb lines being hung at the corners of the shaft to keep the opening vertical.

An act of the Pennsylvania legislature, approved June 30, 1885, regulates the conduct of coal mining in the State so far as the safety of persons employed in and about the mines is concerned. Former acts are consolidated and revised in this, and new provisions are added. By virtue of this act both the anthracite and bituminous coal fields are divided into districts, each of which is placed in charge of an inspector, whose duty it is to see that the provisions of the law are carried out, and to make annual report to the Secretary of Internal Affairs of such facts and statistics as the law requires to be made. As there will be frequent occasion hereafter to refer to various provisions of this act of assembly, it will be mentioned simply as the act of 1885. The matter is brought up here in order that the rule relating to the sinking of shafts, as laid down in the act, may be referred to. These rules provide the manner in which the necessary structures at the mouth of the opening shall be erected, what precautions shall be taken to prevent material from falling into the pit, how the ascent and descent shall be made, that all blasts during the process of sinking shall be exploded by an electric battery, etc. All these rules have but one object, the safety of the workmen.

The horizontal dimensions of the modern shaft average about twelve feet in width by thirty feet in length. This space is divided crosswise, down the entire depth of the shaft, into compartments of which there are usually four. The first of these compartments is the pump way, a space devoted to the pipes, pump-rod, and other appliances connected with the pumping system. To this six feet in breadth is allowed. Then come, in succession, the two carriage ways, each of which may be seven feet wide, and, finally, the air passage through which the foul air is exhausted from the mine, and to which ten feet is appropriated. The partitions between these compartments are made of oak sticks six inches square, called buntons. The ends of the buntons are let into the rock sides of the shaft, and they are placed horizontally at a vertical distance from each other of about four feet. These bunton partitions are then closely boarded down the entire distance. The partition between the hoisting compartment and the airway is not only boarded up, but the boards are matched and are rabbeted together. It is necessary to make as nearly air-tight as possible this way for the passage of air, and where the edges of the boarding meet the rock sides of the shaft the irregularities are carefully filled in with brick and mortar.

Fastened to the buntons at each side of each hoisting compartment are continuous strips of hard wood, from four to six inches square, reaching from the top of the shaft to its bottom. These are the "guides." To each side of the carriage, which raises and lowers men and materials, is fastened an iron shoe, shaped like a small rectangular box without top or ends. This shoe fits loosely on to the guide, slides up and down it, and serves to keep the carriage steady while it is ascending or descending. This invention is due to John Curr of Sheffield, England, who introduced it as early as 1798. The ordinary carriage consists of a wooden platform with vertical posts at the middle of the sides united by a cross-beam at the top, and all solidly built and thoroughly braced. The posts are just inside of the guides when the carriage is in place, and are kept parallel to them by the shoes already mentioned. To the middle of the cross-beam is attached the end of a wire cable, from which the carriage is suspended, and by which it is raised and lowered. On the floor of the platform, which is planked over, a track is built uniform with the track at the foot and head of the shaft, and continuous with it when the carriage is at rest at either place. The mine car is pushed on to the platform of the carriage and fastened there by a device which clings to the axle or blocks the wheels.

At the mouth of the shaft and projecting into

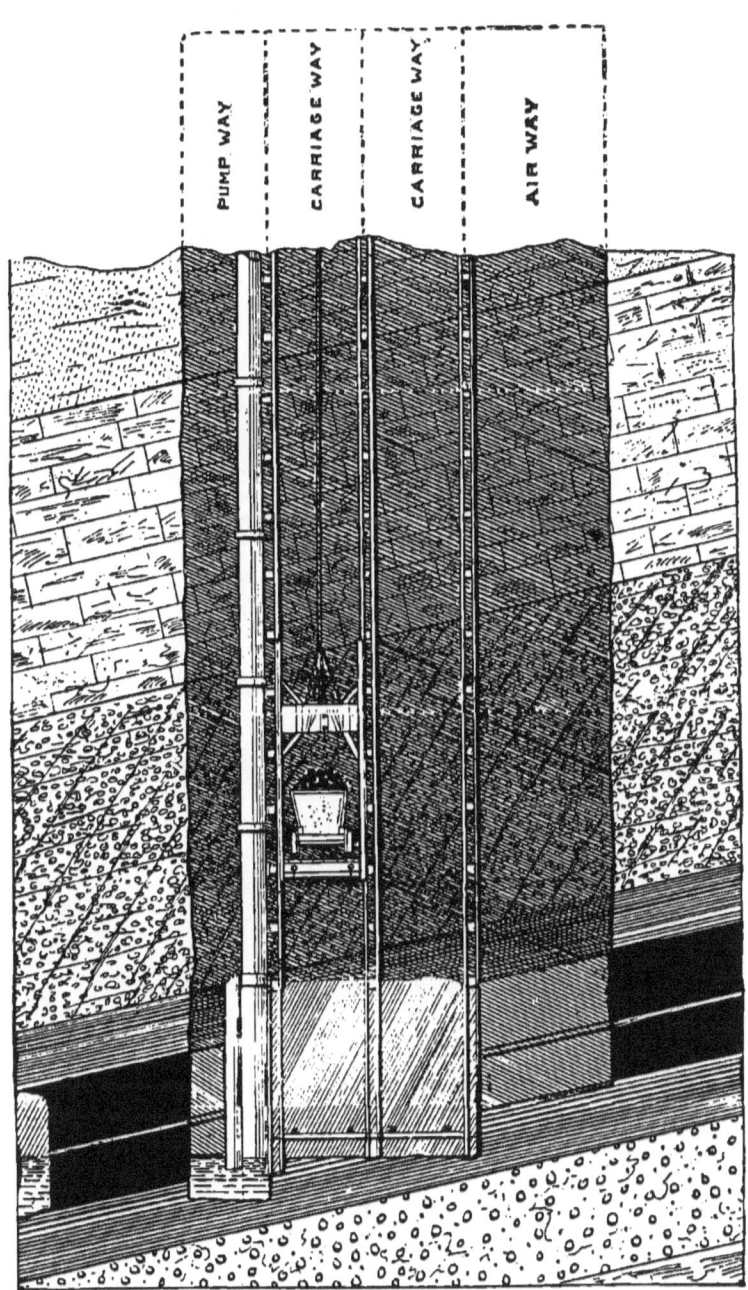

VERTICAL SECTION OF FOOT OF SHAFT WITH ASCENDING CARRIAGE.

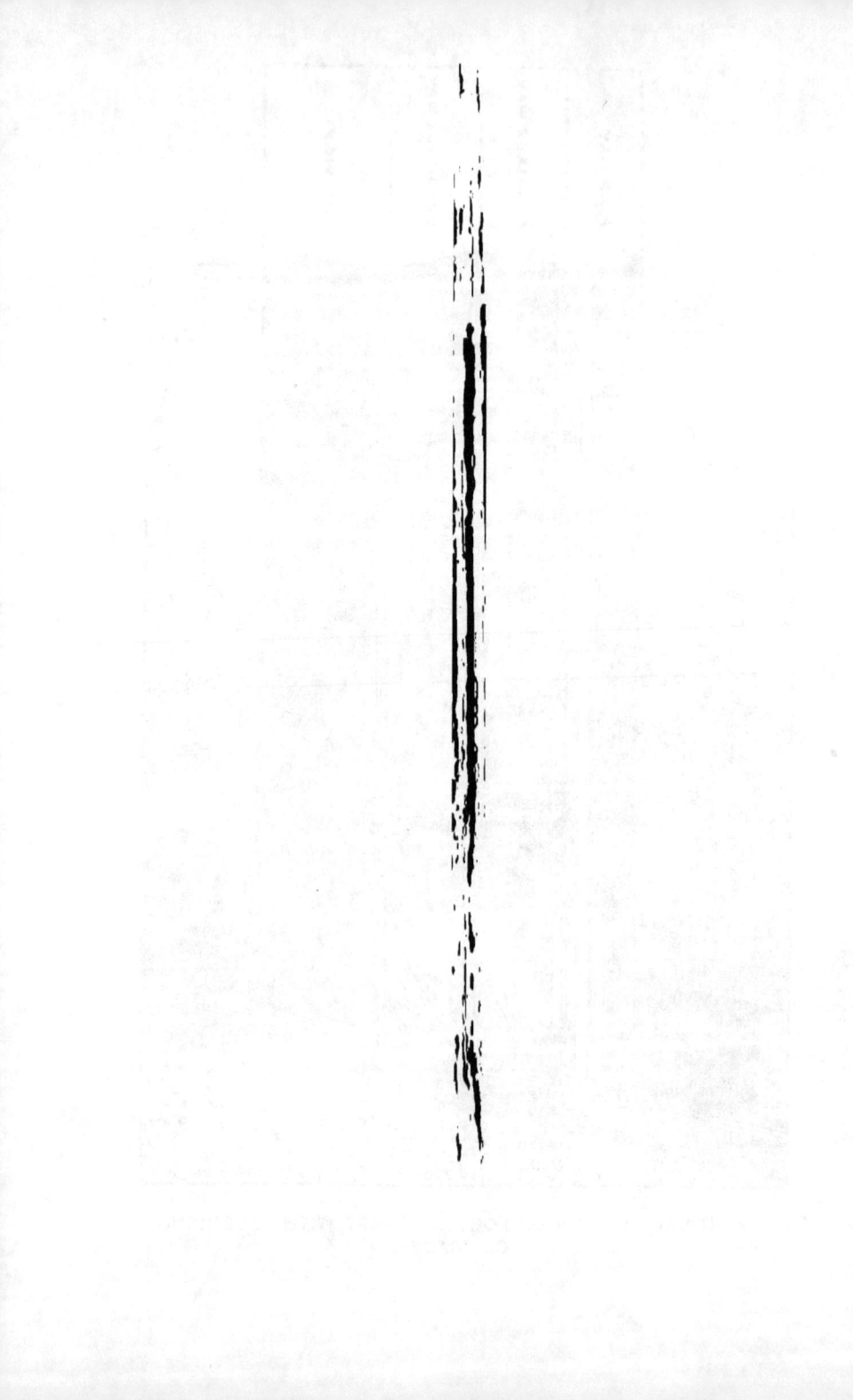

it are the "wings," "keeps," or "cage rests," which are pressed against the sides of the shaft by the ascending carriage, but spring back into place underneath it and support it while it is at rest. When the carriage is ready to descend the wings are withdrawn by hand levers.

The safety carriage is now in general use in at least one hoisting compartment of every shaft. This carriage is built of wrought iron instead of wood; it has a bonnet or roof as a protection against objects falling down the shaft, and it has safety clutches or dogs to stop the carriage and hold it in place in case of accident by breaking ropes or machinery. Operators are required by the act of 1885 to provide safety carriages for the use of their employees, and also to keep movable gates or covers at the mouth of each shaft to prevent persons and materials from falling into the opening.

Where mining is done by shaft there is seldom any other way provided for the passage of workmen in and out than the way by the carriage. A small shaft for the admission of air is sometimes driven down to the highest part of the seam, and ladders are placed in the opening on which men may climb up and down, but these ladders are seldom used save in an emergency. It is made obligatory upon operators, by the act of 1885, to provide two openings to every seam of coal that is being worked; these openings to be at least sixty feet apart underground, and one hundred and fifty feet apart at the surface. The object of this rule is to provide a way of escape for workmen in case of accident to the main outlet.

It is seldom necessary, however, in these days, to sink a separate shaft in order to comply with this provision of the law; the underground workings of the mines having such extensive connections that often not only two but many openings are accessible from each seam.

As to the comparative cost of the different methods of entry, the drift is of course the cheapest. In this method the very first blow of the pick brings down a fragment of coal that may be sent to market and sold. For this reason the sinking of a slope is less expensive than tunneling or shafting, because the excavation is made in the coal. It may be said to cost from twenty-five to fifty dollars per linear yard to sink an ordinary double track slope, from fifty to seventy-five dollars per linear yard to drive a tunnel of average cross-section to accommodate two tracks, and from three hundred to five hundred dollars per linear yard to sink a shaft with four compartments. Of course circumstances, especially the character of strata, may greatly increase or lessen these limits of cost. Indeed, it has happened that a shaft in process of sinking, which had already cost many thousands of dollars, has been necessarily abandoned because an intractable bed of quicksand has been encountered.

The experienced coal operator, knowing the advantages and disadvantages of each of these methods of entering a mine, and the adaptability of each to his particular coal bed, will find no difficulty in making a selection from them. Indeed, there may be, and usually is, practically, no choice. The selection of a site for the opening is ordinarily attended with but little more freedom of choice. The outcrop, if there be one, the topography of the surface, the outline of the coal seam, the accessibility of the spot, the location of the breaker, all govern in the selection of the site, and usually all point to the one most available spot.

CHAPTER VIII.

A PLAN OF A COAL MINE.

The progress that has been made in the science of mining coal within the last half century bears favorable comparison with the progress that has been made in the other industrial sciences. To-day the ripest experience and the best engineering skill in the land are brought to bear upon the problems connected with coal mining. In comparison with the marked ability employed and the marked success attained in the mining enterprises of to-day, the efforts of the early miners are almost amusing. The pick and the wedge were the chief instruments used in getting out coal. Powder was not thought to be available until John Flanigan, a miner for Abijah Smith, introduced it into the mines in 1818. It is said that when openings were first made for coal in the vicinity of Pottsville shallow shafts were sunk, and the coal was hoisted in a large vessel by means of a common windlass. As soon as the water became troublesome, which was usually as soon as the shaft had reached a depth of twenty or thirty feet, this opening was abandoned, a new shaft sunk, and the process repeated.

A PLAN OF A COAL MINE. 95

The mine operator of to-day, having decided upon the shaft as the best method of entry into his mine, sinks it to the bottom of the coal bed, so that its longest dimension shall be with the dip of the seam. Then from each side of the shaft, and at right angles to it, he cuts a passage out through the coal with a width of from ten to fourteen feet. These are the beginnings of the "gangways." Then from each end of the rectangular foot of the shaft he cuts another passage, at right angles to the first one, about six or eight feet wide, and extending to a distance of from fifteen to thirty feet. These are the first "cross-headings." At the extremities of the cross-headings passages are now driven parallel to the gangways. These last passages are called "airways." When the gangways and airways have reached a distance of from sixty to one hundred feet from the foot of the shaft they are united by new cross-headings.

It is now apparent that two pillars of coal, each from fifteen to thirty feet wide and from sixty to one hundred feet long are left on each side of the shaft. Larger pillars than these may be left if the roof about the shaft should need more support. It is also apparent, the coal seam being inclined, that the level of one of the airways is higher than the level of the gangway, and the level of the other airway is lower.

It will be remembered that the design was to sink the shaft so that its foot should be nearly to the bottom of the synclinal valley or basin. If this has been done, then it is possible that the passage below the foot of the shaft parallel to the gangway actually runs along the synclinal axis. But if the bottom of the valley is still lower, the cross-headings will be driven farther down and a new parallel passage made, and, if necessary, still another. These openings now slope from the foot of the shaft downward, and in them is collected not only the water that may fall from the shaft, but, as the work advances, all the water that comes from all parts of the mine. This basin which is thus made to receive the mine water is called the "sump," and from it the water is pumped up through the shaft and discharged at the surface. If the mine happens to be a very wet one it will require the constant labor of the most powerful pumping engine to keep the level of the water in the sump lower than the foot of the shaft. In some cases, in older workings, a section of the mine which has been worked out and abandoned is used for a sump, and then the water may cover an area many acres in extent. When a shaft has been newly sunk, the openings for the sump are the only ones that are made below the level of the foot of the shaft or below the level of the gangway. Henceforth all the workings will be made on the upper side of the gangway, extending up the slope of the seam, until such time as it may be deemed advisable to sink an inside slope to open a new set of workings on a lower level. The main gangway on one side of the shaft and the airway above it are now carried along simultaneously, and parallel with each other, and are united at distances of from forty to sixty feet by cross-headings. As soon as the last cross-heading is opened the one which immediately preceded it is walled up as tightly as possible. This is to insure ventilation. A current of air comes down the hoisting-way of the shaft, passes into the gangway and along it to the last cross-heading, where it crosses up into the airway and traverses the airway back to the cross-heading that was driven up from the upper end of the foot of the shaft. Passing down this cross-heading it comes to the air compartment of the shaft, and is drawn out to the surface by a powerful fan. This is the ventilating system of the mine in its simplest form. It is apparent that if any of the cross-headings nearer to the shaft than the last one should be left open, the air current would take a short course through it up to the airway, and so back to the shaft, without going to the extremity of the gangway at all. This gangway is the main artery of the mine; it is the highway by which all the empty cars go in to the working faces, and by which all the loaded cars come out to the foot of the shaft; it is the general watercourse by which the entire mine above it is drained, and by which the water is carried to the sump. In comparatively flat seams its height is the height of the slate or rock roof of the coal bed, but in steep pitching seams it is made seven or eight feet high with a roof wholly or partly of coal. In some cases the roof and sides are so firm that no timbering is required, and in other cases the timbering must be close and heavy in order to give the necessary support and security. The floor of the gangway must be given a constantly ascending grade, usually from six inches to one foot in every hundred feet, as it is driven inward. This is to facilitate drainage and the movement of loaded cars.

Where the strata are horizontal, or nearly so, as in many of the bituminous mines, the gangway may, and usually does, take a perfectly straight course. This is also true where the line of strike has but a single direction, no matter how steep the pitch of the seam may be. But both of these conditions are so rare in the anthracite regions that one seldom finds a gangway driven for any considerable distance in one direction. The surface of an inclined coal seam is not dissimilar to the surface of one side of a range of small hills. Any one who has seen a railroad track winding in and out along such a range, keeping to the surface of the ground and preserving a uniformity of grade, can understand why, for the same reasons, the gangway must often change direction in following the seam of coal. It must curve in around the valleys and hollows that indent the seam in the same manner that a surface railroad curves in around the depression where some hillside brook runs down to meet the stream, the course of which the railroad tries to follow; and it must strike out around the projections of the seam in the same way in which a surface railroad bends out around the projecting spurs of the hill range along which it runs. But the coal seam is more irregular and more uncertain in its outline than the hillside, and the curves in it are sharper and more varied. The surface railroad too may shorten its route and relieve its curves by bridging its small valleys and cutting through its narrow ridges. For the gangway this cannot be done. As a rule the coal seam must be followed, no matter where it leads. And it often leads in strange courses, — in courses that at times curve back on themselves like a horseshoe and point toward the foot of the shaft. The mining superintendent or engineer never knows in advance just what tortuous course his main artery may take. He cannot go over the ground and stake out his line as a civil engineer does for a surface railway; he must build as he advances, not knowing what the rock and coal may hide in the next foot ahead of him. He must be prepared to encounter faults, fissures, streams of water, diluvial deposits, and every other obstacle known to mining engineers.

There are several systems of laying out a mine for actual working after the gangway has been driven a sufficient distance. The one most commonly in use in the anthracite region is known as the "pillar and breast" system. In the bituminous mines it is called the "pillar and room," and in the mines of Great Britain the "bord and pillar." It will be borne in mind that the mine which is now being described is in the Wyoming region, where the seams are comparatively flat, the entrance usually by shaft, and the method of working is the pillar and breast system. The gangway and airway are not driven far, not more than two or three hundred feet, perhaps, before the openings are made for the larger production of coal. Beginning on the upper side of the airway, at such a distance from the shaft as will leave a reasonably large sustaining pillar, perhaps from sixty to one hundred feet, an opening is made and driven up the seam at right angles to the airway. This opening is called a "chamber" or "breast." In the bituminous districts it is known as a "room." The chamber is usually about twenty-four feet wide, though where the roof is exceptionally good its width may be increased to thirty-six feet. It is not often opened the full width at the airway. Instead of this a narrow passage, large enough to accommodate the mine car track, is driven up to a distance not exceeding fifteen feet, and it is from this point that the chamber is driven up at its full width. This narrow opening can be more easily closed in case it is desired to

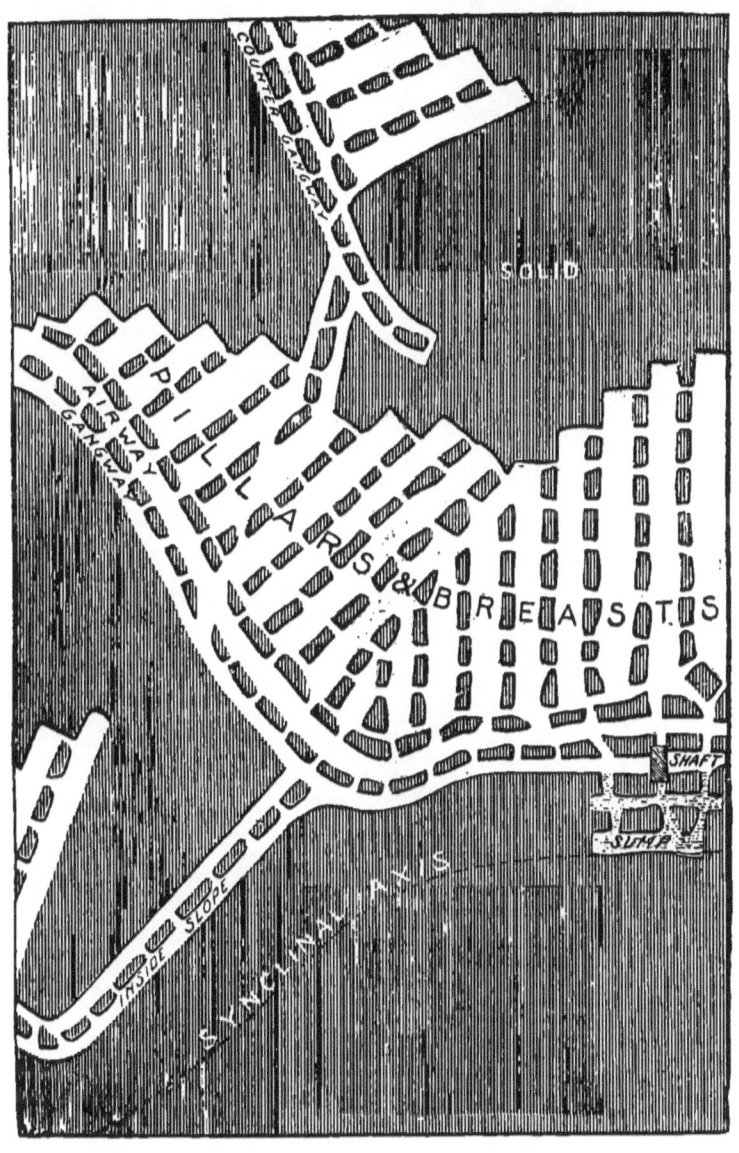

PLAN OF AN ANTHRACITE MINE WITH A SHAFT ENTRANCE.

prevent the passage of air through it, and besides a greater proportion of coal is left in pillars along the airway to prevent the passage from becoming blockaded by falls. When the first chamber has been driven up a distance equal to its width, a new chamber is begun parallel to it and on the side farthest from the shaft. These two chambers are now separated by a wall of coal from fourteen to twenty feet thick. If, however, the workings are deep and there is danger from the weight of superincumbent strata, the wall should be made as thick as the chamber is wide. When the new chamber has been driven to a distance of twenty-five feet, or, if the mine is free from gas and the ventilation is good, to a distance of forty or sixty feet, the wall between the two chambers is pierced by an opening from six to ten feet wide. This is called a cross-heading or "entrance." A partition is now built across the airway between the openings to the two chambers, and the air current is thus forced up into the last chamber, across through the entrance into the first, down it to the airway again, and so in its regular course back to the foot of the shaft. In the mean time progress has been made in the first chamber, and by the time the second chamber has been driven another distance of thirty or sixty feet, the entrance which will then be cut through the wall will find the first chamber still in advance. The inner extremity of the chamber is called the "face." It is sometimes spoken of also as the "breast," though this last name is properly that of the chamber as a whole. The wall of coal at the side of the chamber is called the "rib." A third chamber is now begun and driven up parallel to the other two, then a fourth, a fifth, and so on; as many chambers, indeed, as can be laid off in this way without deviating too greatly from a right angle to the airway. But the face of the first chamber is kept in advance of the face of the second, the face of the second in advance of the face of the third, and so on, until the limit of length is reached. This limit is determined, to some extent, by the dip of the seam. In comparatively flat workings a set of chambers may be driven in to a distance of five hundred, or even six hundred feet. Where the pitch is steep, however, two hundred or three hundred feet is the greatest length at which chambers can be economically worked. The limit of length of chambers is sometimes determined also by an outcrop, an anticlinal axis, a fault, or a boundary line. The wall of coal left between any two chambers is divided by the entrances cut through it into a line of pillars nearly uniform in size. As soon as the second entrance from the airway is cut through the wall the first entrance is blocked tightly up, and as soon as the third entrance is cut through the second is closed, and so on to the extremity of the line of pillars. This is to compel the air current to pass up to the very face of the chamber before it can find a way across to the other chambers and down again into the airway. If the air of the mine is bad, or if the coal is giving off deleterious gases with rapidity, a "brattice" or rude board partition is built from the lower side of the last entrance diagonally up toward the face of the chamber to force the air to the very point where men are working before it finds its way out through an open entrance. These boards are sometimes replaced by a sheet of coarse canvas, called brattice cloth, which is lighter, more easily handled, and answers the same purpose.

From the mine car track in the gangway a branch track is built, crossing the airway and running up each chamber to its face. Up this branch track a mule draws the empty car, and when it is loaded it is let down to the gangway by the miner's laborer. If the dip of the chamber is too steep — more than ten degrees — for a mule to draw the car up, a light car, used only in the chamber and called a "buggy," is pushed up by hand, and when the dip is too steep for this the coal is pushed or allowed to slide down to the foot of the chamber. Chambers are often driven up obliquely in order to reduce the grade, or are curved in their course for the same reason.

When, on account of the steepness of pitch or a change in the direction of the gangway, or for any other reason, one set of parallel chambers is brought to a close, a new set is begun farther along with a different course.

The direction in which a gangway, airway, or chamber is to be driven is fixed by the mine boss. His bearings are obtained with a small miner's compass, and he marks on the roof, near the face of the opening, a chalk line in the direction desired. The miner, sighting back on this line, is thus able to take his course and to keep his opening straight.

Sets of chambers similar to those described are driven up from the gangway along its entire length. This length may be limited by various causes. A boundary line of property, a fault, a thinning out of the coal seam, are some of them. They are usually driven, however, as far as strict principles of economy will allow. A gangway that requires no timbering and is easily kept in good working condition may be driven to a distance of three or four miles. But where these conditions are reversed, a mile may be as great a distance as coal can be hauled through with economy. Beyond that limit it will be cheaper to sink a new shaft or slope than to increase the distance for underground haulage.

As the main gangway progresses inward it may separate into two branches, each following a depression in the coal seam, and these branches may separate into others; so that there may be a number of gangways all keeping the same general level, from each of which sets of chambers are driven. When the chambers tributary to a gangway have reached their limit of length, and there is still an area of coal above them to be mined, a new gangway is opened along the faces of the chambers, or is driven just above them in the solid coal, and from this, which is called a "counter-gangway," new sets of chambers are driven up the seam. It is often necessary to raise and lower cars passing from one gangway to the other on an inclined plane, on which the loaded cars, descending, and attached to one end of a rope, pull up the light cars, ascending and attached to the other end, the rope itself winding around a revolving drum at the head of the plane. This system can be put into use on any incline where the gradient is one in thirty, or steeper.

By this general system of gangways, counter-gangways, airways, chambers, and planes, the area of coal lying on the upper side of the main gangway and on both sides of the shaft is mined out, hauled by mules to the foot of the shaft, and raised to the surface. On long straight gangways the mule is sometimes replaced by a small mine locomotive, and in these later days the electric engine has been introduced into the mines as a hauling agent.

So far, however, in this mine which we are supposed to be working, not a tap of a drill nor a blow of a pick has been made into the coal on the lower side of the gangway save where the sump was excavated at the foot of the shaft. If this shaft has been sunk nearly to the bottom of the basin or synclinal axis, a short tunnel may be driven from the main gangway through the rock or upper bench of coal across the valley to the rise of the seam on the other side. A new gangway may here be driven right and left, and this area of coal be made tributary to the shaft already sunk. It often happens that a large body of coal lies between the main gangway and the synclinal axis, for these two lines may diverge greatly as they recede from the shaft. But chambers cannot be driven down from the main gangway owing to the difficulties of transportation and drainage. It therefore becomes necessary, in order to work this area, to sink a slope from the main gangway down to or toward the synclinal axis, and from the foot of this slope to drive a new gangway. From this new gangway chambers will be opened extending up the seam to the line of the main gangway, but not generally breaking through into it. The coal is run down to the lower level gangway, hauled to the foot of the slope, and hoisted up it to the main gangway. It is apparent, however, that the inclined plane system cannot work here; the conditions are reversed; the loaded cars are drawn up and the light ones are let down. To do this work it is necessary to bring into use a small steam stationary engine, or one working by compressed air. A common method is to locate the steam engine on the surface vertically above the head of the underground slope, and to carry power to the sheaves below by wire ropes running down through bore holes drilled for that purpose.

The system of slope mining by lifts, which is in common use in the Middle and Southern anthracite districts, has been explained in a preceding chapter. In this system the sump is always made by extending the slope a short distance below the level of the gangway. This gangway is driven from the foot of the slope to the right and left in the same manner as in the Wyoming region, except that, the seam being so greatly inclined, the gangway roof, or a part of it at least, will usually be of coal instead of slate or rock, and in very steep pitching seams the airway will be almost vertically above the gangway. The gangway is not usually so crooked as where the workings are flat, and having been started only three hundred feet down the slope from the surface, it often follows the coal to some low point on the line of outcrop, and is then known as a water level gangway, which is practically the same as a drift.

The system of opening and working breasts differs somewhat from that in use in the Northern field. Beginning at such a distance from the foot of the slope as will leave a good thick slope pillar for its protection, a narrow shute is driven up from the gangway into the coal to a distance of perhaps thirty feet, at a height of six feet, and with a width of from six to nine feet. It is then opened out to its full width as a breast and continued up the seam toward the outcrop, not often breaking through to daylight unless an airway or manway is to be made. Parallel breasts are then laid off and worked out by the usual pillar and breast system. If the dip is less than twelve or fifteen degrees, the coal may be run down from the working face in a buggy, dumped on to a platform or into the shute, and loaded thence into a mine car standing on the gangway. If the dip is more than fifteen degrees the pieces of coal will slide down the breast to the shute, though if it is under twenty-five or thirty degrees the floor of the breast should be laid with sheet iron to lessen the friction and give greater facility in movement. In a steep-pitching breast a plank partition is built across the shute just above the gangway, to hold back the coal until it is desired to load a car with it. This partition is called a "battery," or, if there is a similar partition to hold the coal in the breast, a "check battery." In this partition there is an opening through which the coal may be drawn when desired, and through which the men may also go to their work, though a separate manway is often provided. In these steep-pitching breasts the miner works by standing on the coal which he has already mined, and which is held back by the battery, in order to reach the uncut coal above him. There are various systems of shutes, batteries, manways, etc., in use, but all are based on the same principles.

When the gangway of the first lift has reached its limit in both directions, and the breasts from it have been worked up to their limit, the slope is sunk to another distance of three hundred feet, and the process is repeated. From the gangway of the second lift the breasts are not extended up far enough to break through into the gangway above; a wall of coal is left between that gangway and the faces of the breasts, from fifteen to forty feet in thickness, known as the "chain-pillar." This is for the protection of the upper gangway against falls and crushes, and is also necessary to hold back water from escaping into the lower level. These lifts will continue, at distances of about three hundred feet apart, until the synclinal valley is reached.

When the method of opening the mine by a shaft is employed in these steep-pitching seams, the shaft is sunk to the lowest level, and the successive sets of gangways and breasts are laid off as the work progresses upwards; that is, the slope method of extending the lifts downwards is simply reversed.

The method of mining by tunnel and drift, and by slope in the flat workings, is not different from the method already described for shafts. So soon as the drift, tunnel, or slope has extended far enough into the coal seam it becomes a gangway, chambers are laid off from it, and mining goes on in the familiar mode.

Various modifications of the pillar and breast system are employed in the anthracite coal mines, but no system is in use which is radically different.

In the "long wall system," common in Great Britain, and used to some extent in the bituminous mines of Pennsylvania and the Western States, the process of cutting coal is carried on simultaneously along an extended face. The roof is allowed to fall, back of the workers, roads being preserved to the gangway, and the roof at the face is temporarily supported by an abundance of wooden props.

The descriptions of underground workings that have now been given have, of necessity, been very general in their character. It is impossible, in a limited space, to describe the various methods and modifications of methods which are in use. No two mines, even in the same district, are worked exactly alike. Sometimes they differ widely in plan and operation. That system must be employed in each one which will best meet its peculiar requirements. There is large scope here for the play of inventive genius. There is scarcely a mine of any importance in the entire coal region in which one cannot find some new contrivance, some ingenious scheme, some masterpiece of invention devised to meet some special emergency which may have arisen for the first time in the history of mining. Yet the general features of all coal mining methods must of necessity be the same in underground workings. No one reasonably familiar with them could ever mistake a map of a coal mine for a map of anything else under the sun.

CHAPTER IX.

THE MINER AT WORK.

THE number of persons employed in a single mine in the anthracite regions varies from a dozen in the newest and smallest mines to seven hundred or eight hundred in the largest and busiest. The average would probably be between two hundred and three hundred. In the bituminous districts the average is not so large.

First among those who go down into the mine is the mine boss, or, as he is sometimes called, the "inside boss." It is his duty "to direct and generally supervise the whole working of the mine." All the workmen are under his control, and everything is done in obedience to his orders. He reports to, and receives instructions from, the general superintendent of the mines.

Next in authority is the fire boss. It is his duty to examine, every morning before the men come to their work, every place in the mine where explosive gas is evolved or likely to be evolved, and to give the necessary instructions to the workmen regarding the same. He also has general oversight of the ventilating system, and sees that all stoppings, doors, brattices, and airways are kept in proper condition. The driver boss has charge of the driver boys and door boys, and sees that the mules are properly cared for and are not abused. Each driver boy has charge of a mule, and the mule draws the empty cars in along the gangway and up to the faces of the chambers, and draws the loaded cars out to the foot of the shaft. The door boy must stay at his post all day and open and close the door for the cars to pass in and out. The use and necessity of these doors will be explained in a subsequent chapter. Then there are the footmen, carpenters, blacksmiths, masons, and tracklayers, whose occupations in the mines are apparent from the names which indicate their several callings.

Finally we have the miners and the miners' laborers, and it now becomes a matter of especial interest to inquire into the character of their work and their manner of performing it. To drive a gangway or airway is much the same as driving a chamber, except that the gangway is only about one third the width of a chamber, and must be driven on a slightly ascending grade. Gangway driving is special work, for which the miner receives special wages, it being impossible in this work to send out as much coal with the same amount of labor as can be sent out in chamber work. And since the great bulk of coal is taken from the chambers, it will be better to observe in one of them the processes of mining.

There are usually four workmen, two miners and two laborers, employed in each chamber. The miners are employed by, or are under contract with, the coal company, and the laborers are employed by the miners, subject to the approval of the mining superintendent. The two miners divide their profits or wages equally with each other, and are called "butties." A miner's butty is the man who works the chamber with him on halves. A laborer's butty is the man who is associated with him in the employ of the same miners. Between the miner and the laborer there is a well-defined and strictly observed line of social demarcation. The miner belongs to the aristocracy of underground workers; the laborer is of a lower order, whose great ambition it is to be elevated, at an early day, to that height on which his employer stands.

Now as to the work done by these four men. Before the chamber has progressed a pillar's length above the airway, propping will usually be necessary to sustain the roof, so large an area of which has been left without support. Hardwood props about nine inches in diameter are used for the purpose. They are purchased by the mining companies in large quantities, and are usually cut and hauled to the railroad in the winter time to be shipped at any season to the mines. By the law of 1885 the person or company operating a mine is obliged to furnish to the miner, at the face of his chamber, as many props of the required length as he may need. Having received the props the miner himself sets them on each side of the middle line of the chamber at such points as he thinks require them, or at such points as the mine boss designates. He drives the prop to its place by means of a large flat wedge inserted between the top of it and the roof, thus making the stick tight and firm and also giving it a larger bearing against the roof. Some chambers require very few props; others must be well lined with them. Their necessity depends upon the character of the roof. If it is soft, slaty, and loose it must be supported at frequent intervals. It very rarely occurs that a chamber, worked to its limit, has needed no propping from its foot to its face. Usually a good part of the miner's time is occupied in setting props as his work at the face advances.

Every seam has its top and bottom bench of coal, divided about midway by a thin slate partition, and one bench is always taken out to a horizontal depth of four or five feet before the other one is mined. If the upper bench contains the best and cleanest coal, with the smoothest plane of cleavage at the roof, that is first taken out; but if the choice coal lies at the bottom, then the lower bench is first mined. The reason for this is that a shot heavy enough to blast out effectually the section of rough, bony, or slaty coal which sticks to the roof or floor would be heavy enough to shatter the adjoining bench of clean brittle coal, and make a large part of it so fine as to be useless.

Let us now suppose that the miner has a clean, vertical wall of coal at the face of his chamber in which to begin work. Making sure that his tools and materials are all at hand, he first takes up his drill. This is a round or hexagonal iron bar about one and an eighth inches in diameter, and about five and a half feet long, tipped at the working end with steel. This end is flattened out into a blade or chisel, having a slight concave curve on its edge, and being somewhat wider at its extremity than the diameter of the bar. At the other end of the drill the diameter is increased to one and a half inches, forming a circular ridge at the extremity of the bar, in one side of which ridge a semicircular notch is cut into the face of the drill. The use of this notch will be subsequently explained. This, then, is the tool with which the miner begins his work. Selecting the bench to be first mined he chooses a point a few feet to the right or left of the middle line of the face and delivers upon it the first stroke with the sharp edge of his drill; and as he strikes successive blows he rotates the drill in his hands in order to make the hole round. The drill is never struck on the head with sledges. Its cutting force depends on the momentum given to it in the hands of the miner, and the stroke made by it is a jumping or elastic stroke.

Instead of the bar drill, which has been described, many of the miners use a machine hand-drill for boring holes. This machine works upon the same principle that the jackscrew does. It is operated by hand by means of a crank, and an auger-like projection forces its way into the coal. The work of turning the crank is more laborious than that of drilling with the bar-drill, but the extra labor is much more than compensated for by the greater speed at which boring is done. It is probably due to the spirit of conservatism among miners that this machine is not in general use by them. Coal-cutting machines, working by steam or compressed air, are not used in the anthracite mines. The character of the coal, the thickness of the seams, and the inclination of the strata make their employment impracticable.

When the hole has been drilled to a depth of about four and a half feet it is carefully cleaned out with a scraper. This is a light iron rod with a handle on one end of it and a little spoon, turned up like a mustard spoon, on the other end. Then the cartridge is inserted and pushed in to the farther extremity of the hole. The cartridge is simply a tube made of heavy manila paper formed over a cartridge stick, filled with black powder, and folded at the ends. Dynamite and other high explosives are not used, because they create too much waste. Ready-made cartridges in jointed sections are largely used, but as a rule the miner makes his own cartridge as he needs it.

The miner's needle is an iron rod about five and

one half feet in length, with a handle at one end. It is about five eighths of an inch in diameter at the handle end, and tapers to a point at the other end. When the cartridge has been pushed in to the extreme end of the bore hole, the needle is inserted also, the point of it piercing the outer end of the cartridge. The needle is then allowed to rest on the bottom or at the side of the drill hole while the miner gathers fine dirt from the floor of the mine, dampens it slightly if it is dry, and pushes it into the hole alongside. This dirt is then forced in against the cartridge with the head of the drill. More dirt is put in and driven home, and still more, until, by the time the hole is filled to its outer extremity, the packing is hard and firm. This process is called tamping. It can now be seen that the semicircular notch on the rim of the blunt end of the drill is for the purpose of allowing the drill to slip along over the needle, which still retains its position, and at the same time to fill the diameter of the hole. The tamping being finished the miner takes hold of the needle by the handle, turns it once or twice gently in its bed, and then slowly withdraws it. A round, smooth channel is thus left from the outside directly in to the powder of the cartridge, and into this channel the squib is inserted. The squib is simply an elongated fire-cracker. It has about the diameter of a rye straw, is about four inches in length, and its covering projects an inch or two at one end and is twisted up for a fuse. The covering of the squib may indeed be of straw, sometimes it is of hempen material, but more often, in these days, it is made of paper. It is filled with powder and is then dipped into a resinous mixture to make it water-proof, to coat over the open end so that the powder shall not run out, and to make the wick at the other end mildly inflammable. If the bore hole should be very wet an iron or copper tube, through which the needle is run, is laid to the cartridge before the hole is tamped, and when the needle is withdrawn the squib is inserted into the mouth of the tube. If inflammable gases are exuding from the coal through the bore hole, or if for any other reason it is feared that the cartridge will be exploded too quickly, a short piece of cotton wick, dipped in oil, is attached to the fuse of the squib to lengthen it, and this extra section of fuse is allowed to hang down from the mouth of the bore hole against the face of coal.

When all is ready the tools are removed to a safe distance, a lighted lamp is touched to the fuse, the men cry "Fire!" to warn all who may be in the vicinity, and, retreating down the chamber, they take refuge behind some convenient pillar. The fuse burns so slowly that the men have ample time in which to get out of harm's way, if ordinary care is taken. When the fire reaches the powder in the squib the same force that propels a fire-cracker or a rocket acts upon the squib and sends it violently through the channel or tube into contact with the powder of the cartridge. The explosion that results throws out a section of coal from the face, breaking it into large pieces. So soon as the place has settled after the firing of the shot the men go back to the face to note the result. The broken coal is pushed to one side, and preparations are made for drilling the next hole. It usually takes five shots to break down a single bench. When both benches of coal have been blasted out the length of the chamber has been increased by five or six feet. In blasting, the miner must take advantage of such conditions as are presented to him at the face of the working, and he will bore his hole and fire his shot where, in his judgment, the best result will be attained. He cannot always take one position at his drilling; it is rarely that he finds a comfortable one. Sometimes he must hold the drill at arm's length above his head, at other times he must rest on his knees while working, still oftener he is obliged to lie on his back or side on the wet floor of the mine, and work in that position, with occasional respite, for hours at a time.

In nearly every chamber the miner has a powder chest which he keeps locked, and which is stored at some safe and convenient place, not too close to the face. In this chest he keeps, besides his powder, his cartridge paper, cartridge pin, squibs, lamp-wick, chalk, and such other little conveniences and necessaries as every workingman must have at hand. The other tools are usually at the face. He has there a mining pick. This pick is straight and pointed, and from the head or eye, where the handle enters, it will measure about nine inches to each end. It is used for bringing down slate and coal from roof, ribs, and face. The bottom pick is used by the laborer for breaking up the coal after it is down. This pick measures about two feet from tip to tip, and is curved slightly upward at the points. Each miner has two drills, and perhaps a hand machine-drill. He has also a steel crowbar for prying down loose portions of the roof, and for turning heavy pieces of slate or coal. He has an eight-pound steel hammer, with a handle two feet and four inches in length, which he uses in setting props; and he has a heavy sledge for breaking rock and coal. The list is completed by three large scoop shovels, used generally to shovel the smaller pieces of broken coal from the floor of the chamber into the mine car.

The miner must furnish his own tools. His powder, fuse, and oil he gets from the company that employs him, and they are charged to him in the account that is stated between them monthly. It will not do to omit the miner's lamp from the list of appliances used in his calling; it is too great a necessity. Without it he could do absolutely nothing; he could not even find his way to his chamber. Formerly candles were much used in the mines; in Great Britain they are still common; but the anthracite miner invariably uses a lamp. This is a round, flat-bottomed tin box, about the size of a small after-dinner coffee cup. It has a hinged lid on top, a spout on one side, and a handle shaped like a hook with the point down on the opposite side. By this hooked handle the lamp is fastened to the front of the miner's cap, and he wears it so at his labor, removing it only for the purpose of renewing the material in it, or of approaching the powder chest, or of examining more closely some portion of his work. In the lamp he burns crude petroleum, which is fed from a cotton wick emerging from the spout. Very recently electricity has been introduced into the gangways of some large mines, for lighting purposes, and has given great satisfaction. Perhaps the day is not far distant when an electric light will swing from the roof at the face of every working chamber.

When the coal has been blasted down and the props have been set the miner's work is done; the rest belongs to the laborers. They must break up the coal, load it into the cars, run it down to the gangway, pile up the refuse, and clear the chamber for the next day's work. The mine carpenters have laid a track, consisting of wooden rails set into caps or notched ties, as far up the chamber as the working at the face would permit. Up this

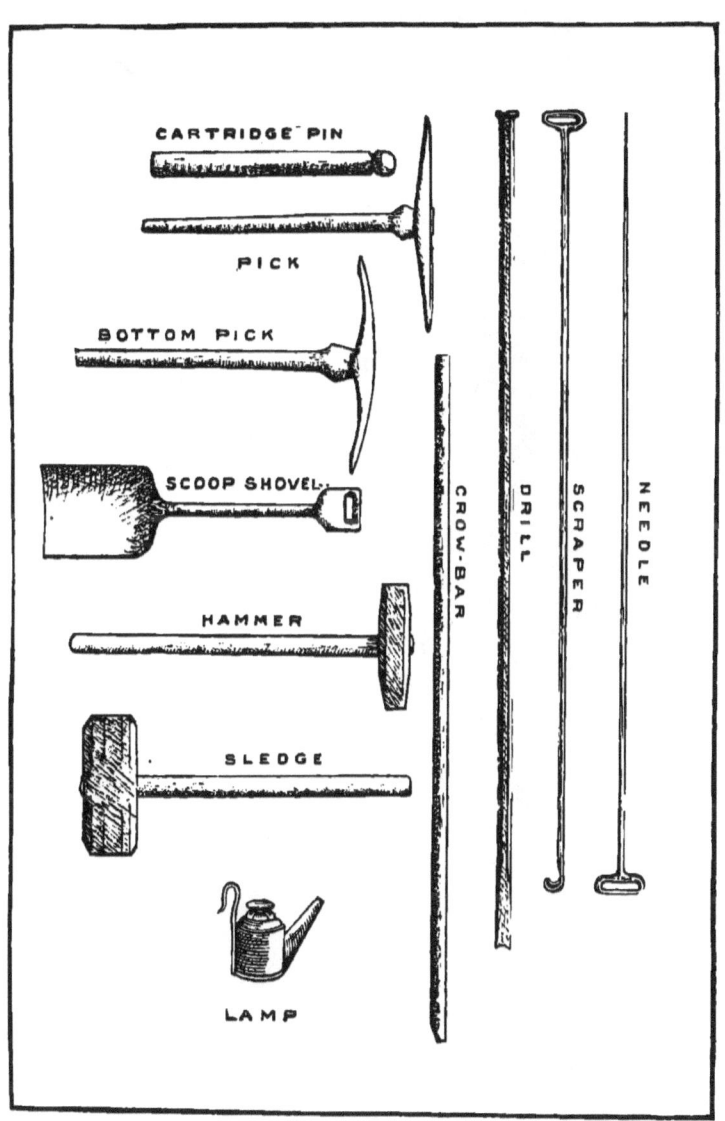

MINER'S TOOLS.

track the mule and driver boy have brought the empty car and left it at the face. The laborers throw into it first the smaller pieces of coal which they shovel up from the floor of the chamber, then huge chunks are tumbled in and piled skillfully on top until the car is almost overbalanced with its load. It is then pushed out to the gangway to await the coming of the driver boy, who attaches it to his trip of loads and takes it to the shaft.

The mine car is usually but a smaller edition of the coal cars that can be seen any day on the surface railways of the country. The running portion is of iron, and the box is stoutly built of hardwood, braced and stiffened by iron tie-rods, bolts, and shoes. At the end of the car is a vertical swinging door, hung from the top by an iron rod, which crosses the box. This door is latched on the outside near the bottom, and the coal is dumped from the car by tipping it up and letting the unlatched door swing outward. The size of the car depends greatly on the size and character of the workings in which it is used. Perhaps an average size would be ten feet long, five feet wide, and five feet high from the rail. Such a car would contain about one hundred cubic feet, and would hold from two and one half to three tons of coal. The track gauges in common use vary by three inch widths from two feet and six inches to four feet. The miner and laborer start to their work in the morning at six o'clock. If they enter the mine by shaft they must go down before seven o'clock, for at that hour the engineer stops lowering men and begins to hoist coal. Immediately after arriving at the face of his chamber the miner begins to cut coal. If the vein is thick and clean, if his shots are all effective, and if he has good luck generally, he will cut his allowance of coal for the day by ten or eleven o'clock in the forenoon. It will be understood that by the system in use by most of the coal companies not more than a certain number of carloads may be sent out from each chamber per day. And when the miner has blasted down enough coal to make up that number of loads his day's work is done. It is very seldom indeed that he is not through before two o'clock in the afternoon. But he never stays to assist the laborer. It is beneath his dignity as a miner to help break up and loah the coal which has been brought down by means of his judgment and skill. So the laborer is always last in the chamber. His work is seldom done before four or five o'clock in the afternoon. He has just so much coal to break up, load, and push down to the gangway, no matter how successful the miner may have been. He consoles himself, however, by looking forward to the time when he shall himself become a miner.

Blasting is always a dangerous occupation, and the law in Pennsylvania, embodied in the act of 1885, has recognized its especial danger in the mines, by making certain provisions concerning it for the protection of life and limb. The rules laid down are strict and complete, yet, in spite of them, accidents from powder explosions and premature blasts are frequent and destructive. But it must be said that these accidents are due, in most part, to violations of these rules. It is impossible for colliery authorities to keep constant watch over the workmen in every chamber. The conduct of these men must be largely governed by themselves, and the frequency of accidents, both serious and fatal, as a result of carelessness on the part of workmen, does not seem to deter other workmen from constantly running the same risks. The most prevalent and the most serious source of danger to the miner is not, however, in blasting, but in falls of coal, slate, and rock from the roof, ribs, and face of the chamber. Material that has become loosened by blasting is pulled down carelessly, or falls without warning. In many cases the roof is insufficiently propped, and large sections of it give way. Men are caught under these falling masses every day, and are either killed outright or seriously injured. Yet, as in the case of blasting, their injuries are largely the result of their own carelessness. Any one who reads the reports of these cases cannot fail to be convinced of this fact. The mine inspector's reports of Pennsylvania show that during the year 1887 there were in the anthracite district three hundred and thirteen fatal accidents which occurred in and about the mines. Of this number one hundred and forty-seven were due to falls of roof and coal, while only twenty-one were caused by explosions of blasting material. These figures indicate plainly the direction in which the skill and supervision of operators and the care and watchfulness of workmen should be exerted for the protection of life.

CHAPTER X.

WHEN THE MINE ROOF FALLS.

A FIRST visit to a coal mine will be prolific of strange sights and sounds and of novel sensations. If one enters the mine by a shaft, the first noteworthy experience will be the descent on the cage or carriage. The visitor will probably be under the care of one of the mine foremen, without whose presence or authority he would not be allowed to descend, and indeed would not wish to. From the head to the foot of every shaft a speaking tube extends, and signaling apparatus, which is continued to the engine-room. These appliances are required by law. In these days the signals are often operated by electricity. At the head of the shaft is stationed a headman and at the foot of the shaft a footman, whose assistants aid in pushing cars on and off the carriages. The footman is notified of your coming, and you take your place on the empty safety carriage. It swings slightly as you step on to it, just enough to make you realize that you have passed from the stable to the unstable, and that besides the few inches of planking under your feet, there is nothing between you and the floor of the mine, five hundred feet or more below you. When all is ready the foreman cries: "Slack off!" the signal to the engineer is given, the carriage is slightly raised, the wings are withdrawn, and the descent begins. If the carriage goes down as rapidly as it ordinarily does your first sensation will be that of falling. It will seem as though that on which you were standing has been suddenly removed from beneath your feet, and your impulse will be to grasp for something above you. You will hardly have recovered from this sensation when it will seem to you that the motion of the carriage has been reversed, and that you are now going up more rapidly than you were at first descending. There will be an alternation of these sensations during the minute or two occupied in the descent, until finally the motion of the carriage becomes suddenly slower, and you feel it strike gently at the bottom of the shaft. As you step out into the darkness nothing is visible to you except the shifting flames of the workmen's lamps; you cannot even see distinctly the men who carry them. You are given a seat on the footman's bench near by until your eyes have accommodated themselves to the situation. After a few minutes you are able to distinguish objects that are ten or fifteen feet away. You can see through the murky atmosphere the rough walls of solid coal about you, the flat, black, moist roof overhead, the mine car tracks at your feet. The carriages appear and disappear, and are loaded and unloaded at the foot of the shaft, while the passage, at one side of which you sit, is filled with mine cars, mules, and driver boys in apparently inextricable confusion. The body of a mule looms up suddenly in front of you; you catch a glimpse of a boy hurrying by; a swarthy face, lighted up by the flame of a lamp gleams out of the darkness, but the body that belongs to it is in deep shadow, you cannot see it. Bare, brawny arms become visible and are withdrawn, men's voices sound strange, there is a constant rumbling of cars, a regular clicking sound as the carriage stops and starts, incessant shouting by the boys; somewhere the sound of falling water. Such are the sights and sounds at the shaft's foot. If now you pass in along the gangway, you will be apt to throw the light of your lamp to your feet to see where you are stepping. You will experience a sense of confinement in the narrow passage with its low roof and close, black walls. Occasionally you will have to crowd against the rib to let a trip of mine cars, drawn by a smoking mule, in charge of a boy with soiled face and greasy clothes, pass by. Perhaps you walk up one of the inclined planes to a counter gangway. You are lucky if you are in a mine where the roof is so high that you need not bend over as you walk. The men whom you meet have little lamps on their caps, smoking and flaring in the strong air current. You can see little of these persons except their soiled faces. Everything here is black and dingy; there is no color relief to outline the form of any object. Now you come to a door on the upper side of the gangway. A small boy jumps up from a bench and pulls the door open for the party to pass through. As it closes behind you the strong current of air nearly extinguishes your lamp. You walk along the airway for a little distance, and then you come to the foot of a chamber. Up somewhere in the darkness, apparently far away, you see lights twinkling, four of them. They appear and disappear, they bob up and down, they waver from side to side, till you wonder what strange contortions the people who carry them must be going through to give them such erratic movements. By and by there is a cry of "Fire!" the cry is repeated several times, three lights move down the chamber toward you and suddenly disappear, then the fourth one approaches apparently with more action, and disappears also. The men who carry them have hidden behind pillars. You wait one, two, three minutes, looking into darkness. Then there is a sudden wave-like movement in the air; it strikes your face, you feel it in your ears; the flame of your lamp is blown aside. Immediately there is the sound of an explosion and the crash of falling blocks of coal. The waves of disturbed air still touch your face gently. Soon the lights reappear, all four of them, and advance toward the face. In a minute they are swallowed up in the powder smoke that has rolled out from the blast; you see only a faint blur, and their movements are indistinct. But when the smoke has reached and passed you the air is clearer again, and the lights twinkle and dance as merrily as they did before the blast was fired. Now you go up the chamber, taking care not to stumble over the high caps, into the notches of which the wooden rails of the track are laid. On one side of you is a wall, built up with pieces of slate and bony coal and the refuse of the mine, on the other you can reach out your hand and touch the heavy wooden props that support the roof, and beyond the props there is darkness, or if the rib of coal is visible it is barely distinct. Up at the face there is a scene of great activity. Bare-armed men, without coat or vest, are working with bar and pick and shovel, moving the fallen coal from the face, breaking it, loading it into the mine car which stands near by. The miners are at the face prying down loose pieces of coal. One takes his lamp in his hand and flashes its light along the black, broken, shiny surface, deciding upon the best point to begin the next drill hole, discussing the matter with his companion, giving quick orders to the laborers, acting with energy and a will. He takes up his drill, runs his fingers across the edge of it professionally, balances it in his hands, and strikes a certain point on the face with it, turning it slightly at each stroke. He has taken his position, lying on his side perhaps, and then begins the regular tap, tap, of the drill into the coal. The laborers have loaded the mine car, removed the block from the wheel, and now, grasping the end of it firmly, hold back on it as it moves by gravity down the chamber to the gangway. You may follow it out, watch the driver boy as he attaches it to his trip, and go with him back to the foot of the shaft.

You have seen something of the operation of taking out coal, something of the ceaseless activity which pervades the working portions of the mine. But your visit to the mine has been at a time when hundreds of men are busy around you, when the rumble, the click, the tap, the noise of blasting, the sound of human voices, are incessant. If you were there alone, the only living being in the mine, you would experience a different set of sensations. If you stood or sat motionless you would find the silence oppressive. One who has not had this experience can have no adequate conception of the profound stillness of a deserted mine. On the surface of the earth one cannot find a time nor a place in which the ear is not assailed by noises; the stirring of the grasses in the field at midnight sends sound-waves traveling through space. Wherever there is life there is motion, and wherever there is motion there is sound. But down here there is no life, no motion, no sound. The silence is not only oppressive, it is painful, it becomes unbearable. No person could be long subjected to it and retain his reason; it would be like trying to live in an element to which the human body is not adapted. Suppose you are not only in silence but in darkness. There is no darkness on the surface of the earth that is at all comparable with the darkness of the mine. On the surface the eyes can grow accustomed to the deepest gloom of night. Clouds cannot shut out every ray of light from hidden moon or stars. But down in the mine, whether in night-time or daytime, there is no possible lightening up of the gloom by nature; she cannot send her brightest sunbeam through three hundred feet of solid rock. If one is in the mines without a light, he has before him, behind him, everywhere, utter blackness. To be lost in this way, a mile from any opening to-day, in the midst of a confusion of galleries, in an abandoned mine, and to be compelled to feel one's way to safety, is a painful experience, is one indeed which the writer himself has had.

There comes a time in the history of every mine when it is pervaded only by silence and darkness. All the coal that can be carried from it by the shaft or slope or other outlet has been mined and taken out, and the place is abandoned. But before this comes to pass the work of robbing the pillars must be done. This work consists in breaking from the pillars as much coal as can possibly be taken without too great risk to the workmen. The process is begun at the faces of the chambers, at the farthest extremity of the mine, and the work progresses constantly toward the shaft or other opening by which the coal thus obtained is taken out. It can readily be seen that robbing pillars is a dangerous business. For so soon as the column becomes too slender to support the roof it will give way and the slate and rock will come crashing down into the chamber. The workmen must be constantly on the alert, watchful for every sign of danger, but at the best some will be injured, some will perhaps be killed, by the falling masses from the roof. Yet this work must be done, otherwise coal mining would not be profitable, the waste would be too great. The coal that can be taken out under the prevailing systems will average only fifty per cent. of the whole body in the mine, and at least ten per cent. more will be lost in waste at the breaker, so that it behooves a company to have its pillars robbed as closely as possible. It is after all this has been done, and all tools and appliances have been removed from the mine, that it is abandoned. Perhaps the lower levels of it become filled with water. It is a waste of crushed pillars, fallen rock, and blocked passages. Indeed, it is difficult to conceive of anything more weird and desolate than an abandoned mine. To walk or climb or creep through one is like walking with Dante through the regions of the lost. There are masses of rock piled up in great confusion to the jagged roof, dull surfaces of coal and slate, rotting timbers patched here and there with spots of snow-white fungus, black stretches of still water into which a bit of falling slate or coal will strike and send a thousand echoes rattling through the ghostly chambers. For a noise which on the surface of the earth will not break the quiet of a summer night, down here will almost make your heart stand still with fear, so startling is it in distinctness.

But it is not only in abandoned mines that falls of roof take place, nor yet alone at the unpropped face of breast or gangway. They are liable to occur at almost any point in any mine. Sometimes only a small piece of slate, not larger perhaps than a shingle, will come down; again the roof of an entire chamber will fall. It is possible that two or more chambers will be involved in the disturbance, and instances occasionally occur in a working mine where a fall covers an area many acres in extent. The falls that are limited in extent, that are confined to a single chamber or the face of a chamber, do not interfere with the pillars and can be readily cleared away. They are due to lack of support for the roof, to insufficient propping and injudicious blasting, and may, to a great extent, be guarded against successfully by care and watchfulness. But to foresee or prevent the more extended falls is often impossible. They are due to the general pressure of overlying strata over a considerable area, and both props and pillars give way under so great a strain. Sometimes they come without a moment's warning; usually, however, their approach is indicated by unmistakable signs days or even weeks in advance of the actual fall. There will be cracks in the roof, small pieces of slate will drop to the floor, the distance between floor and roof will grow perceptibly less, pillars will bulge in the middle and little fragments of coal not larger than peas will break from them with a crackling sound and fall to the floor, until a deposit of fine coal is thus formed at the base of each pillar in the infected district. This crackling and falling is known as "working," and this general condition is called a "crush" or a "squeeze." If one stands quite still in a section of a mine where there is a squeeze, he will hear all about him, coming from the "working" pillars, these faint crackling noises, like the snapping of dry twigs under the feet. Sometimes the floor of underclay or the roof of shale is so soft that the pillar, instead of bulging or breaking, enters the strata above or below as the roof settles. When this occurs it is called "creeping." In the steep-pitching veins the tendency of the pillars on the approach of a squeeze is to "slip," that is, to move perceptibly down the incline. When these indications occur the workmen are withdrawn from the portion of the mine which is "working," and vigorous measures are taken to counteract the pressure, by props and other supports placed under the roof. Sometimes this work is effectual, sometimes it is of no avail whatever. Often the fall comes before the first prop can be set; and when it comes the crash is terrible, the destruction is great. However, not many feet in thickness of the roof strata can come down; the slate and rock which first fall are broken and heaped in such irregular masses on the floor that they soon extend up to the roof and afford it new and effectual support. It is therefore only near the outcrop, or where the mine is not deep, that a fall in it disturbs the earth at the surface. But in the mining of the upper veins such disturbances were frequent. In passing through the coal regions one will occasionally see a depression, or a series of depressions, in the earth's surface to which his attention will be attracted on account of their peculiar shape. They are not often more than ten or fifteen feet in depth, and though of irregular outline their approximate diameter seldom exceeds sixty feet. They are the surface indications of a fall in shallow mines, and are known as "caves" or "cave holes." A section of country one or more acres in extent may, however, be so strewn with them as to make the land practically valueless.

When the upper vein in the Wyoming region was being mined, buildings on the surface were occasionally disturbed by these falls, but not often. If houses had been erected over a shallow mine before the coal was taken out, strong pillars were left under them to support the roof, and if the mining had already been done and the pillars robbed, no one would risk the erection of a building over a place liable to fall, for these places were known, and points above them on the surface could be definitely located. Sensational stories are sometimes started concerning a mining town or city that it is liable any night, while its inhabitants are asleep, to be engulfed in the depths of some mine, the vast cavities of which are spread out beneath it. It is almost unnecessary to say that such dangers are purely imaginary. There is probably not a town or city in the mining districts so located that a single stone of it in the populated portion would be disturbed by a fall in the mines underneath it, supposing there were mines underneath it, and that a fall is liable to take place in them. The areas of surface which could possibly be disturbed by a fall are too limited in extent, and are too well known, to make such a general catastrophe at all within the possibilities. The mines in the upper coal seams have for the most part been worked out and abandoned long ago, and the roof rock has settled into permanent position and rigidity. In the deep mines of the present day no fall, however extensive, could be felt at the surface. The broken masses of roof rock that come down first would have filled up the cavities and supported the strata above them, long before any perceptible movement could have reached the surface. The conditions that lead to surface falls in the Middle and Southern regions are somewhat different from those that prevail in the Wyoming field. In the first-mentioned districts steep-pitching coal seams are the rule, and they all come to the surface in lines of outcrop. In driving breasts up from the gangway of the first level, it is intended to leave from ten to twelve yards of coal between the face of the breast and the outcrop; while over the outcrop will be from twelve to twenty feet of soil. Any experienced miner can tell when the face of the breast is approaching the outcrop; the coal becomes softer, changes in color, breaks into smaller pieces, sometimes water runs down through. It is obviously unsafe to erect buildings on the line of this outcrop, or immediately inside of it, where the roof is thin. There is no assurance that the body of coal left will not slip down the breast; and the pillars of coal near the surface are so soft that any disturbance of this kind may cause them to give way and let down the entire thickness of strata above them. This was what occurred at the Stockton mines near Hazleton on December 18, 1869. Two double tenement houses were situated over the face of a worked-out breast, near the outcrop. About five o'clock in the morning the roof fell, carrying both houses down with it a distance of about eighty feet into the old breast. The inhabitants of one of the houses escaped from it a moment before it went down, those in the other house, ten in number, were carried into the mine, and were killed. The buildings in the pit took fire almost immediately, and rescue of the bodies crushed there among the débris was impossible.

Accidents of this class are happily very rare. The exercise of ordinary judgment is sufficient to prevent them. The list of disasters due to falls of roof at the faces of chambers might, as has already been explained, be greatly reduced by the same means. But it is often impossible to prevent, or even to guard against, those falls which cover a large area, though their coming may be heralded for days by the working of pillars and all the indications of a squeeze. This was the case at the fall in the Carbondale mines in 1846, one of the most extensive falls that has ever been known. It covered an area of from forty to fifty acres, fourteen persons were killed by it, and the bodies of eight of them were never recovered. Although this disaster occurred more than forty years ago, the writer had the privilege, in the summer of 1888, of hearing an account of it from one of the survivors, Mr. Andrew Bryden. Mr. Bryden is now, and has been for many years, one of the general mining superintendents for the Pennsylvania Coal Company, with headquarters at Pittston, Pennsylvania. His story of the fall is as follows: "This disaster occurred on the twelfth day of January, 1846, at about eight o'clock in the fore-

A GANGWAY.

noon. It was in Drifts No. 1 and No. 2 of the Delaware and Hudson Canal Company's mines at Carbondale. The part of the mine in which the caving in was most serious was on the plane heading, at the face of which I was at work. We heard the fall; it came like a thunderclap. We felt the concussion distinctly, and the rush of air occasioned by it put out our lights. I and those who were working with me knew that the fall had come, and we thought it better to try immediately to find our way out, although we had no idea that the fall had been so extensive or the calamity so great. We did not doubt but that we should be able to make our way along the faces of the chambers, next to the solid coal, to an opening at the outcrop; so we relighted our lamps and started. We had gone but a little way before we saw the effects of the tremendous rush of air. Loaded cars had been lifted and thrown from the track, and the heavy walls with which entrances were blocked had been torn out and the débris scattered through the chambers. We began then to believe that the fall had been a large one, but before we reached the line of it we met a party of twenty-five or thirty men. They were much frightened, and were running in toward the face of the heading, the point from which we had just come. They said that the entire mine had caved in; that the fall had extended close up to the faces of the chambers along the line of solid coal, leaving no possible means of escape in the direction we were going; and that the only safe place in the entire section was the place which we were leaving, at the face of the heading. This heading having been driven for some distance into the solid coal, the fall could not well reach in to the face of it. We were greatly discouraged by the news that these men told us, and we turned back and went with them in to the face of the heading. We had little hope of being able to get out through the body of the fall, — the way in which we did finally escape, — for we knew that the mine had been working, and that the roof had been breaking down that morning in the lower level. Indeed, we could hear it at that moment cracking, crashing, and falling with a great noise. We felt that the only safe place was at the face of the heading where we were, and most of the party clung closely to it. Some of us would go out occasionally to the last entrance to listen and investigate, but the noise of the still falling roof was so alarming that no one dared venture farther. After a long time spent thus in waiting I suggested that we should start out in parties of three or four, so that we should not be in each other's way, and so that all of us should not be exposed to the same particular danger, and try to make our way through the fall. But the majority of the men were too much frightened to accede to this proposition; they were determined that we should all remain together. So when some of us started out the whole body rushed out after us, and followed along until we came to the line of the fall. We had succeeded in picking our way but a short distance through the fallen portion of the mine when we met my father, Alexander Bryden, coming toward us. He was foreman of the mine. We heard him calling us out before he reached us, and you may be sure that no more welcome sound ever struck upon our ears. He was outside when the fall came, but the thunder of it had scarcely ceased before he started in to learn its extent, and to rescue, if possible, the endangered men. He had not gone far when he met three men hastening toward the surface, who told him how extensive and dreadful the calamity had been, and urged him not to imperil his life by going farther. But my father was determined to go, and he pushed on. He made his way over hills of fallen rock, he crawled under leaning slabs of slate, he forced his body through apertures scarcely large enough to admit it, he hurried under hanging pieces of roof that crashed down in his path the moment he had passed; and finally he came to us. I have no doubt that he was as glad to find us and help us as we were to see him. Then he led us back through the terrible path by which he had come, and brought us every one beyond the fall to a place of safety. When we were there my father asked if any person had been left inside. He was told that one, Dennis Farrell, was at the face of his chamber, so badly injured across his spine that he could not walk. The miners in their retreat to the face of our heading had found him lying under a heavy piece of coal. They had rolled it off from him, but seeing that he could not walk they set him up in the corner of his chamber, thinking it might be as safe a place as the one to which they were going, and gave him a light and left him. My father asked if any one would go in with him and help carry Dennis out, but none of them dared to go; it was too dangerous a journey. So my father made his way back alone through the fallen mine, and found the crippled and imprisoned miner. The man was totally helpless, and my father lifted him to his back and carried him as far as he could. He drew him gently through the low and narrow passages of the fall, he climbed with him over the hills of broken rock, and finally he brought him out to where the other men were. They carried him to the surface, a mile farther, and then to his home. Dennis and his brother John were working the chamber together, and when the piece of coal fell upon Dennis his brother ran into the next chamber for help. He had scarcely got into it when the roof of the chamber fell and buried him, and he was never seen again, alive or dead.

"It was only a little while after we got out before the roof fell in on the way we had come and closed it up, and it was not opened again for a year afterward. But we knew there were others still in the mine, and after we got Farrell out my father organized a rescuing party, and kept up the search for the imprisoned miners night and day.

"John Hosie was in the mine when the fall came. He was one of the foremen, and he and my father were friends. Two days had passed in unavailing search for him, and it was thought that he must have been crushed under the rock with the rest. But on the morning of the third day my father met him face to face in one of the desolate fallen portions of the mine. He was in darkness, he was almost exhausted, his clothing was in rags, and his fingers were torn and bleeding. When he saw my father he could give utterance to only two words: 'Oh, Bryden!' he said, and then his heart failed him and he cried like a child. He had been caught in the fall and had lost his light, and though he was familiar with the passages of the mine he could not find his way along them on account of the débris with which they were filled, and the utter confusion into which everything had been thrown. He had wandered about for two days and nights in the fallen mine, clambering over jagged hills of rock, digging his way, with torn fingers, through masses of wreckage, in constant peril from falling roof and yawning pit, hungry, thirsty, and alone in the terrible darkness. What wonder that his heart gave way in the moment of rescue!

"The bodies of some of those who were shut in by the fall, or buried under it, were found when the drift was again opened, but for others the mine has been an undisturbed grave for more than forty years."

CHAPTER XI.

AIR AND WATER IN THE MINES.

MAN is an air-breathing animal. So soon as his supply of air is cut off he dies. In proportion as that supply is lessened or vitiated, his physical and mental energies fail. One of the first requisites, therefore, in all mining operations is that the ventilation shall be good. To accomplish this end an air current must be established. It is true that into any accessible cavity atmospheric air will rush, but if it be allowed to remain in that cavity without any replacement it becomes dead and unfit to breathe. If, in addition to this, it takes up deleterious gases, like those which escape from the coal measures, it becomes poisoned and dangerous to human life. Hence the necessity of a continuous current. Provisions for such a current are made with the opening into every mine. The separate air compartment of a shaft has already been noticed. In drifts, tunnels, and slopes a part of the opening is partitioned off for an airway, or, what is more common, a separate passage is driven parallel with, and alongside of, the main one. In drifts and tunnels, since the mines there are not deep, air shafts are often driven at some other point above the workings, or slopes are sunk from the outcrop to accommodate the return air from the mine. It is due to the necessity of maintaining an air current that all passages and chambers are driven in pairs or sets in the manner already explained. It has also been explained how the fresh air going in at the carriage ways of the shaft, or other openings, passes along the gangway to its extremity, back along the airway, up to and across the faces of each set of chambers, and then down into the airway again, to be carried to the foot of the shaft and up by the air passage to the surface. But in the larger mines there are many passages besides the main gangway that must be supplied with air, and the current must therefore be divided or split to accommodate them; so these separate currents, taken in this way from the main current, and themselves often divided and subdivided, are called "splits." The air channels thus branching, uniting, crossing, and recrossing form a most complicated system of ventilation. But the current goes nowhere by chance. Every course is marked out for it. On the fact that it follows that given path depends the lives of the workmen and the successful operation of the mine. Sometimes it becomes necessary to carry two currents of air through the same passage in opposite directions. In that case the passage will either be partitioned along its length, or a wooden box laid through it to conduct one of the air currents. If one air course crosses

AIR AND WATER IN THE MINES. 149

another, as is often the case, a channel will be cut in the roof of one of the passages, and the lower side of the channel will be closed tightly by masonry, to prevent any possible intermingling of the currents, a circumstance which might prove disastrous. Entrances and cross-headings cut through between parallel passages for purposes of ventilation are closed as soon as the next cross-heading is made, for reasons already explained. This closing is usually done by building up in the aperture a wall of slate, rock, and coal, and filling the chinks with dirt from the floor of the mine. Sometimes wooden partitions are put in instead, and between principal air passages the cross-headings are closed by heavy walls of masonry. When it is necessary to turn the air from any traveling way, or to prevent it from further following such traveling way, a partition is built across the passage, and in the opening left in the partition a door is swung. If this is across a way through which mine cars pass, a boy will be stationed at the door to open it when the cars come and close it as soon as they have gone through. He is called a "door boy." All doors are so hung as to swing open against the current of air, and are therefore self-closing. The law directs that this shall be done. There are several patented devices for giving an automatic movement to mine doors; but few if any of them are in practical operation in the anthracite mines. The conditions here are not favorable for the use of self-acting doors, and besides this the act of 1885 provides that all main doors shall have an attendant. The law is very explicit on this subject of ventilation; it is a matter of the utmost importance in operating a mine. A failure of the air current for even an hour might, in some mines, result in the death of all those who chanced to be inside. For this current not only supplies air for breathing purposes, but it takes up the smoke, the dust, the dangerous and the poisonous gases, and carries them to the surface. In the same way pure air is drawn into the lungs, loaded with the refuse matter brought there by the blood, and then expelled. So life is preserved in both cases.

In order to create this circulation of air and make it continuous, artificial means are ordinarily used. The earliest method of creating an artificial air current which should be constant, and one still in use to a limited extent, is that by the open furnace. This is an ordinary fireplace with grate bars, built near the foot of an opening into the mine, and having a bricked-in smoke-flue which leads into the air passage of that opening at some little distance above the floor of the mine. The volume of heat thus passing into the airway will rarefy the air therein, and so create and maintain a strong, invariable, upward current. Sometimes the furnace is placed at the foot of an air shaft a long distance from the main opening, thus making it an upcast shaft. The reverse, however, is usually the case.

All air that enters the mine by any opening is usually drawn out at the main shaft or other main entrance. But as the air returning from the working places of the mine is often laden with inflammable gases, it is not allowed to come into contact with the fire of the furnace, but is carried into the shaft by a channel cut into the rock above the roof of the mine. Furnace ventilation in mines in which explosive gases are generated is dangerous at the best, and is now prohibited by the act of 1885.

The modern and most common method of creating and maintaining a circulation of air in a mine is by a fan built at the mouth of the air compartment of the shaft or slope. The fan exhausts the air from the mine by the airway, and fresh air rushes in by the carriage way, or any other opening to the surface to restore the equilibrium. Sometimes the fan is used as a blower and forces air into the mine instead of exhausting it. The advantage of this method is that it gives better air to the workmen at the faces of chambers and headings, but the objection to it is that it brings all the smoke and gases out by the main gangway. This is a serious objection, not only making this principal passage unfit to see or breathe in, but making it dangerous also by the presence of inflammable gases. The fan is therefore commonly used as an exhauster.

There are various kinds of fans in use at the

mines, but the kind generally employed is patterned after Guibal's invention. It is simply a great wheel without a rim, and instead of spokes it has blades like those of a windmill. It is run by a steam-engine, makes forty revolutions per minute at an average rate of speed, and sends from one hundred thousand to two hundred thousand cubic feet of fresh air per minute into the mine.

The act of 1885 requires the mine operator to furnish two hundred cubic feet of air per minute to every man in the mine. This is the maximum amount necessary for perfect respiration. In the larger workings perhaps six hundred men and boys are employed. For this number one hundred and twenty thousand cubic feet of air per minute would be required by law. A large fan would supply this amount by running at almost its minimum rate of speed. So long, therefore, as the fan and air passages are in good working condition there need be no fear of lack of proper ventilation. But to give absolutely pure air to the workers in the mine is an utter impossibility under any system that has yet been devised. The outer atmosphere that is drawn into the mines has hardly got beyond the light of the sun before it has taken up a certain percentage of impurities. As it passes by the working faces of the chambers it carries along with it the gases evolved from the coal; principally the carbonic acid gas or black damp, and the light carbureted hydrogen or fire damp. It also takes up and carries along the powder smoke, the organic matter contained in the exhalations of men and animals, the products of decaying timber, and the dust which is always in the air. Nor is this the only deterioration which this air current undergoes. The proportion of oxygen in it is diminished by the burning of many lamps, by the respiration of many men, and by the constant decay of wood. It is seen, therefore, that the air in which the miner must breathe is far from being the pure oxygen and hydrogen of the outside atmosphere. It follows also that the longer the route is of any particular current, and the more working faces it passes in its course, the more heavily laden will it be with impurities, and the more poisonous for those men who last breathe it on its return to the upcast air shaft.

This evil, however, is limited in extent by the act of 1885, which provides that no more than seventy-five persons shall be employed at the same time in any one split or current of air.

The wonder is that the health of these mine workers does not sooner fail them, especially when we take into consideration the wet condition of many of the mines. It is a fact, however, that miners as a class are not more subject to disease than other workmen. The decimation in their ranks is due mostly to accidents producing bodily injuries and death, not to diseases which attack them as a result of their occupation.

Next in importance to the matter of ventilation in mines is the matter of drainage. The first difficulty experienced from water is while the shaft or slope is in process of sinking. It is usually necessary to hold the water in one side of the opening while work is going on in the other side. A small pumping engine is generally sufficient to keep the pit clear until the bottom is reached, but occasionally the amount of water is such that a large engine and pumping appliances have to be put in place at once. In Europe much trouble is often experienced from the excessive flow of water while sinking the shaft, and a watertight casing has frequently to follow the shaft downward in order that work may go on at all. Such appliances are not as a rule necessary in this country, though much difficulty has been encountered in sinking shafts through the quicksand deposits of the Susquehanna basin in the Wyoming valley.

The general principle of mine drainage has been already explained. It is, in brief, that the floor of the mine shall be so graded that all water will gravitate to a certain point. That point is near the foot of the shaft or slope, and is at the mouth of the drift or tunnel. But from the sump of the shaft or slope the water must be raised by artificial means. A powerful steam pumping engine, located at the surface, is employed to do this work, and one compartment of the shaft or slope, known as the pump-way, is set aside for the accommodation of pipe, pump-rods, and supporting timbers, which extend from the top to the bottom of the shaft. The most powerful of these pumps will throw out a volume of twelve hundred gallons of water per minute. It is seldom that the tonnage of water pumped from a mine falls below the tonnage of coal hoisted, and in some of the wet collieries of the Lehigh district eight or ten tons of water are pumped out for every ton of coal hoisted. In the Wyoming district a thousand tons of water a day is not an unusual amount to be thrown out of a mine by a single pump.

In driving gangways or chambers toward abandoned workings that have been allowed to fill with water much care is necessary, especially if the new mine is on a lower level, which is usually the case. The act of 1885 provides that "whenever a place is likely to contain a dangerous accumulation of water, the working approaching such place shall not exceed twelve feet in width, and there shall constantly be kept, at a distance of not less than twenty feet in advance, at least one bore hole near the centre of the working, and sufficient flank bore holes on each side." It often happened, before accurate surveys of mines were required to be made and filed, that operators would drive chambers or gangways toward these reservoirs of water in ignorance of their whereabouts. The firing of a blast, the blow of a pick, perhaps, would so weaken the barrier pillar that it would give way and the water breaking through would sweep into the lower workings with irresistible force, carrying death to the workmen in its path and destruction to the mine. Some very distressing accidents have occurred in this way. It is customary now for operators, when approaching with their workings a boundary line of property, to leave a barrier pillar at least one hundred feet thick between that line and the outer rib or face of their workings; and this whether the area on the other side of the line is or is not worked out. Under the present system of accurate surveying and mapping, accidents resulting from flooding by mine water should be rare, since the location of boundary lines may be calculated almost to the inch, as well as the location of all workings in their relation to each other.

But accidents due to a flooding by surface water are not always to be obviated. Sometimes when a stream crosses the line of outcrop the water will break through into the mine and flood the lower levels in an incredibly short space of time; and this too when good judgment and prudence have been used in leaving sufficient coal for protection. The continuity and character of the strata lying between the earth's surface and the coal face cannot always be determined. It is not often that accidents from flooding occur while mining is going on under large bodies of water. The precautionary measures taken in presence of a known danger are sufficient to reduce that danger to a minimum.

Disasters occur occasionally as the result of a peculiarly deceptive condition of the overlying strata, whereby a rush of earth, quicksand, or mud into a mine causes loss of life and destruction of property. The bed of a stream cut deep into the rocks in some former geological period, and then filled to the level of the surrounding country with drift in some later age, leaves a dangerous and unsuspected depression in the strata which the miner's drill may pierce or his blast break into at any time with disastrous results. One of the most characteristic of this class of accidents occurred at Nanticoke in the Wyoming region on the 18th of December, 1885, in a mine operated by the Susquehanna Coal Company. A miner by the name of Kiveler broke into a depression of this kind while blasting, and immediately through the aperture a great volume of water, quicksand, and culm came rushing down. It filled up that entire portion of the mine, burying twenty-six men and boys beyond possible hope of rescue and endangering the lives of hundreds of others. Energetic efforts were made to tunnel through the masses of sand and culm packed in the passages of the mine in order to reach those whose avenues of escape had been cut off, many believing that they had been able to reach high enough ground to escape the flood. These efforts, lasting through many weeks, were wholly unsuccessful. The men were never reached. Bore holes, drilled into the chambers where they were imprisoned, both from the inside and from the surface, proved conclusively that the passages were crowded full of sand and culm, and that the men must have perished immediately upon the occurrence of the disaster.

CHAPTER XII.

THE DANGEROUS GASES.

One of the chief dangers to which workmen in the mines are subject arises from the gases given off by minerals and metals. Though these deleterious gases are commonly found in more or less abundance in the coal mines, and are usually considered in connection with such mines, they are, nevertheless, not confined to the coal measures. They have been noticed also in mines of lead, sulphur, salt, and other substances. It is said that anthracite contains a much larger proportion of these gases than do bituminous or other coals, but that being hard it holds them more tenaciously, and is therefore worked with less risk. The soft coals, on the contrary, being porous as well as soft, allow the gases to escape from them much more readily, and so increase the danger at the working faces of the mines. The gas given out most abundantly by the coal is light carbureted hydrogen, known as marsh gas, from the fact that being a product of vegetable decomposition under water, bubbles of it rise to the surface on stirring the waters of a marsh. This is the gas that is known to miners as fire damp. The French call it grisou. Marsh gas, in its simple form, consists of four parts of hydrogen to one of carbon. It is about one half the weight of air, and therefore rises and gathers at the roof of a mine chamber, extending downward as it accumulates. When it is mixed with from four to twelve times its volume of atmospheric air it becomes violently explosive. If the mixture is above or below this proportion it is simply inflammable, burning without explosive force, with a pale blue flame. The value of a perfect ventilating current across the faces of chambers which are making gas rapidly can now be appreciated. It is not only necessary that the supply of air should be sufficient to make the gas non-explosive, but that it should be sufficient to dilute it beyond even the point of inflammability. For to its inflammable more than to its explosive quality is due most of the disasters with which it is accredited. A peculiar and dangerous feature of this gas is that it does not always escape from the coal at a uniform rate, but often comes out suddenly in large compact bodies. These are called "blowers." They are found most commonly in faults, in cracks in the coal seams, or in open spots in the body of coal, where they have opportunity to accumulate. They contain, besides marsh gas, less than one per cent. of carbonic acid, and from one to four per cent. of nitrogen. It is impossible to anticipate their coming; the miner's drill may strike into one and free it at any time without a moment's warning. It may even burst through the face by its own power. In such cases danger is imminent, disaster is most common.

When the naked light of the miner comes into contact with any considerable quantity of fire damp in an explosive state the shock that follows is terrific. Men and mules, cars and coal, are hurled together to destruction. Walls are swept out, iron rails are bent double, doors are torn from their fastenings, the mine is laid waste. The damage which results from an explosion of gas is of course much greater than that which is due to mere ignition and burning without the explosive force. In the latter case, however, the danger to the miner is but slightly diminished. He is liable to receive injuries which may prove immediately fatal. His burning lamp no sooner touches the body of fire damp than it bursts into flame, which, propelled by expansive force, passes swiftly down along the roof of the chamber. Taking up enough oxygen from the atmospheric air to make combustion more fierce, it returns to the face of the chamber with a violent contractile surge, scorching everything in its path, and then, perhaps after another brief sally, it burns itself out.

The miner who accidentally fires a block of fire damp falls suddenly flat on his face on the floor of the mine, burying his mouth, nose, and eyes in the dirt to protect them from the flame and intense heat. Then he clasps his hands over the back of his head and neck to protect these parts from injury, and lies waiting for the minute or two to pass before the fire shall have burned itself out. But he must not wait too long. The fatal after damp follows quick upon the heels of the flame, and his only safety from certain death lies now in immediate flight.

The danger from inflammable gases was known and appreciated very early in the history of mining. But it was long thought to be an unavoidable danger. Light must be had or no work could be done, and the only light that could be obtained was from the flame produced by combustion. Candles were commonly used. They were stuck into a ball of clay and fastened to the sides of the working places at the most advantageous points. The bituminous mines of England were peculiarly prolific of inflammable gases; accidents were almost of daily occurrence. On the 25th of May, 1812, a great disaster occurred at Felling Colliery, near Newcastle, in which eighty-nine persons lost their lives by explosion of fire damp, and public attention and the public conscience were directed to the matter of safety in mines more intensely than ever. Sir Humphrey Davy was then in the zenith of his fame. In April, 1815, he returned to London after a triumphal tour through France and Italy, in which his progress had been marked by a series of brilliant experiments. He had no sooner reached home than he was asked by Mr.

Buddle, a well-known colliery owner of that day, to turn his attention toward improved methods of lighting the mines. Specimens of the dangerous gas were sent to him from Newcastle, and he experimented with them. He found that the flame from them would not pass through a small tube, nor through a set of small tubes standing side by side. He found also that the length of the tube was immaterial. He therefore shortened them until they were mere sections, until his set of parallel tubes became simply wire gauze. The proper proportion between the substance of the wire and the size of the aperture was found to be twenty-eight wires to the linear inch, and seven hundred and eighty-four apertures to the square inch, a proportion that is still in use. This wire gauze was then made into the form of a cylindrical tube about six inches long and one and one half inches in diameter, with a flat gauze top. To the bottom of this tube was fastened a small cylindrical oil vessel, and to the top a ring handle. The wick extended up from the oil vessel inside the tube.

When Sir Humphrey had perfected his lamp to a point of safety he took it and went with Mr. Buddle down to Newcastle, and together they traversed with impunity some of the most dangerous parts of the Bentham seam, at that time one of the most fiery coal beds known. At about the same time the celebrated George Stephenson also invented a safety lamp similar in most respects to the Davy, so also, later, did Clanny and Museler, and all four kinds are in general use. Other styles have been invented also, but for the purposes to which a safety lamp is properly applied the Davy doubtless still excels all others. Those purposes are principally the investigation of workings to discover the presence of gas, and to aid in the erection of proper appliances for driving it out. It is not necessary, in these days of powerful ventilating machinery, to allow dangerous gases to remain in working places and to mine the coal there by the light of safety lamps. It is far safer, and better in every way, to sweep the chambers clean from foul air by strong ventilating currents, so that the miner may work by the light of his naked and most convenient common tin lamp. The objection, therefore, to the Davy lamp, that the light given out by it is too dim, need not be considered a serious one. The size of the flame cannot be increased without destroying the proportion between it and the gauze cylinder, and the size of the cylinder cannot be increased without making a dangerously large chamber for the accommodation of explosive gas. Therefore the light given out must, of necessity, be. dim.

But the safety lamp itself must be used with care and prudence, otherwise it may become no less an instrument of danger than the naked lamp. When it is carried into a chamber that contains fire damp the gas enters freely through the gauze into the cylindrical chamber, and is there ignited and consumed without communicating its flame to the outside body. The presence of gas is indicated by the conduct of the flame of the lamp. If the percentage of marsh gas is small the flame simply elongates and becomes smoky. If it is mixed with from eight to twelve or fourteen times its volume of atmospheric air the flame of the wick disappears entirely, and the interior of the cylinder becomes filled with the blue flame of burning gas. It will not do to hold the lamp long in this mixture, the wires will become red with heat, and the outer gas may then become ignited from them. Neither will it do to hold the lamp in a current of gaseous air moving at a greater rate of speed than six or eight feet per second, since in that case the flame is apt to be driven through the gauze and to set fire to the gas outside. There is also danger if the lamp be thrust suddenly into an explosive mixture that the force of the explosion inside the wire-gauze cylinder will force the flame through the mesh. It will be seen, therefore, that even the safety lamp is not an absolute protection against danger from explosive and inflammable gases.

The position and duties of the fire boss at each colliery have already been referred to. He goes into the mine about four o'clock in the morning and makes his round before the men arrive. If gas has been found in an inflammable or explosive condition the workmen are not allowed to enter the place until it has been cleared out by the erection of brattices and other ventilating appliances. If only an insignificant quantity has been found in any chamber, the miner who works the place is warned of its existence and told to brush it out. In obedience to this order he goes to the working face, sets his lamp on the floor, and removing his coat swings that garment vigorously over his head, thus mixing and diluting the gas and driving it down into the current.

It is not in the working chambers, however, that the most dangerous accumulations of fire damp are found, but in the worked out and abandoned portions of the mine. Here it may collect unnoticed until large bodies of it are formed, and then when some one blunders into it with a naked lamp a terrific explosion is the inevitable result. The act of 1885 recognizes this especial danger, and makes it obligatory on operators to keep old workings free of dangerous bodies of gas; and to this end it directs that they shall be inspected at least once a week by the fire boss or his assistant. Where it is known that such gas exists, or is liable to accumulate in old workings, the entrances to such places are barred across, and the word "Fire!" is written conspicuously at the opening to them. But notwithstanding all rules and precautions, ignitions and explosions of fire damp are still dangerously common. Among the thousands of mine workers there is always some one who is careless, some one who blunders; the lessons of perfect watchfulness and obedience are hard lessons to be learned.

As has already been intimated, the danger which results from the burning of fire damp lies not alone in the fierce flame given forth, but also, and perhaps in a still greater degree, in the product of its combustion. This product is known to the miner as "after damp," and consists principally of carbonic acid gas with some nitrogen. It is irrespirable, and a single inhalation of it, in its pure state, will produce immediate insensibility and speedy death. It is heavier than atmospheric air and therefore falls to the bottom of the mine as soon as it is formed from the combustion of the light carbureted hydrogen. It is for this reason that the miner, who has fallen on his face on the floor of the mine to escape the flame of the burning fire damp, rises as soon as that flame has disappeared and hastens, if he is able, to a place of safety. Indeed, it is easier to protect one's self from the surging fire above than from the invisible and insidious gas below, so quickly does it form, so deadly is it in effect.

One of the most characteristic disasters of recent times, resulting from the explosion of fire damp and the accumulation of after damp, occurred on Monday, August 14, 1871, at the Eagle Shaft, situated about a mile below the town of Pittston, in Luzerne County, Pennsylvania. At nine o'clock on the morning of that day a driver boy by the name of Martin Mangan was passing along an upper gangway, driving a mule with a trip of mine cars. Just above him lay a section of the mine that had been worked out and abandoned, in the old chambers of which a large body of fire damp had been allowed to accumulate. At the hour mentioned there came a sudden and extensive fall of roof in these old workings. The impulse given to the air by this fall drove it out into the working galleries, and with it the inflammable gas. When the fire damp reached the heading and touched the flame of Martin Mangan's lighted lamp there was a terrific explosion. At the mouth of the shaft timbers were cracked, clouds of dust poured out, and débris from the mine was thrown violently into the outer air. People who were a mile away heard the noise of the explosion and hastened to the scene. Mining experts knew at once what had occurred. As soon as sufficient repairs could be made to the shaft a rescuing party, led by Superintendent Andrew Bryden of the Pennsylvania Coal Company's mines, descended into the mine and began to search for victims. Those workmen who were on the other side of the shaft from where the explosion took place were rescued and brought out alive. But little progress could be made, however, toward the region of the trouble on account of the after damp which had accumulated. Up to two o'clock on Tuesday morning five dead bodies had been discovered, and during that day twelve more were taken out; all who had worked in that section of the mine. The positions of these bodies showed that the men had fallen where they chanced to be when the explosion occurred. The first wave of after damp that touched them had made them insensible, and death speedily followed. They died from asphyxia.

"Black damp" is pure carbonic acid gas, containing two parts of oxygen to one of carbon. It is the principal constitutent of after damp, which may, indeed, contain no other elements in appreciable quantities. The two mixtures are therefore often spoken of as being the same, and the miners apply the term "choke damp" indiscriminately to either.

Black damp is also given off by the coal in the same manner that fire damp is, and frequently the two mixtures are evolved together. Carbonic acid gas is also one of the products of burning coal, of burning oil, and of the respiration of man and beast. It is about one and a half times as heavy as air, and is therefore always found next to the floor of the mine. This gas is not inflammable. Its presence may be detected by the conduct of the flame of the lamp. In an atmosphere containing but a small percentage of it the lamp light will grow dim, and, as the proportion of gas increases, will become more and more feeble until it is finally extinguished. An atmosphere containing from eight to ten per cent. of this gas may be breathed without immediate danger; it will simply occasion dullness of intellect and numbness of body. This condition changes into one of insensibility as the inhalation continues, or as the percentage of gas is increased, and to enter an undiluted body of it means sudden death. It is stated that the workmen in the Creuzot mine, in France, descended the shaft one morning, on their way to work, not knowing that carbonic acid had formed in the mine during the night. Following one after another along the main passage, they had reached a point not far from the foot of the shaft when the leader suddenly entered into a body of black damp and fell, stricken with asphyxia, before he could utter a cry. The man following him fell also. The third, bending over to draw his comrade out of danger, was himself prostrated, and the fourth, by reason of a similar effort, shared the fate of the others. But the fifth, being an experienced master miner, turned quickly in his tracks and obliged those behind him to ascend the shaft. The black damp is thus quick and terrible in its effect. The greatest danger from it, however, exists, not at the working faces, where it is usually swept away in the ventilating current, but in abandoned workings, where it often accumulates unnoticed.

"White damp" is a more dangerous gas than

either of the others, but is not so frequently found. It is carbonic oxide, and consists of equal portions of carbon and oxygen. It is a very little lighter than air, and has a tendency to rise. When present in a sufficiently pure state it burns with a blue flame, but ordinarily it is incombustible and produces no effect upon the flame of the lamp. It is tasteless and odorless, and its presence cannot be detected before it has done its dangerous work. To breathe an atmosphere containing a very small percentage of it will speedily produce a fatal result. It acts on the system as a narcotic, and its effect is produced even more quickly than is that of black damp. It is not thought to be given off in appreciable quantities by the coal at the open faces; but it is formed when the carbonic acid passes through any ignited carbonaceous material, or when steam passes over burning coal. It is therefore produced most frequently by smouldering gob fires, by burning wood in the mines, or by a shaft on fire, and may exist as one of the results of an explosion of fire damp or of blasting powder. It is the most to be dreaded of any of the gases which the miner has to encounter. He may possibly avoid the surging flame of the fire damp, he may escape from the falling after damp, and make his way unharmed through bodies of black damp lying thick about his feet, but if he has still to encounter this terrible white damp his good fortune will have been of little avail; death will almost surely seize him.

In connection with this may be mentioned the fact that under certain conditions coal dust may become violently explosive. When it is mixed with air, with or without the presence of fire damp, and is set into sudden and intense vibration by a heavy powder blast, a fall of roof, or other means, it may explode with greater destructive force than even fire damp is capable of. Happily such explosions are not frequent, all the conditions necessary being rarely present at the same time. It is obvious, moreover, that an accident of this kind could occur only in a very dry mine. It is true also that the dust of bituminous coals is much more liable to be explosive than the dust of anthracite. No well authenticated instances of coal dust explosions have been reported from the anthracite regions, while in mining soft coals they have undoubtedly occurred. Two cases of this kind were reported from France, one in 1875 and one in 1877. No longer ago than November 9, 1888, a terrible explosion of coal dust occurred in a bituminous coal mine at Pittsburg, Kansas, by which more than one hundred lives were lost.

In some mines the inflammable and poisonous gases are given off in such abundance by the coal that it is dangerous to remain in them for even an hour after ventilation has been stopped. At such collieries when, on account of accident, or for any reason, the fan stops running, the men are called out immediately, and are not allowed to enter again

THE DANGEROUS GASES. 173

until a new circulating current has been established. One of the most notable mine disasters of recent years was caused by the quick accumulation of black damp and white damp in a mine, the ventilating system of which had been destroyed and the shaft burned out by fire. This was at Avondale, near Plymouth, in Luzerne County, Pennsylvania, on the 6th of September, 1869. There were three conditions here, the presence and coöperation of which made this calamity possible. First, the mine was ventilated by a furnace at the foot of the shaft; second, the breaker was built over the mouth of the shaft; and, third, the shaft was the only outlet from the mine. The partition of the ventilating flue took fire from the furnace draught. At ten o'clock in the forenoon a young man by the name of Palmer Steele stepped on the carriage with a load of hay to take to the inside stables. Half way down the shaft the hay took fire from the burning buntons. The engineer saw the flames rise from the mouth and let the carriage, with the young man on it, as quickly as possible to the bottom. There were then in the mine one hundred and eight men. Not one of them came out from it alive. In an incredibly short space of time the flames leaped to the top of the breaker, one hundred feet from the ground, and by the middle of the afternoon the great building was a mass of ruins, covering over and blocking up the only entrance to the mine. It was far into the night before the débris had been sufficiently cleared away to permit of descent into the shaft. Then two men, Thomas W. Williams and David Jones, went down to search for the imprisoned miners. They were scarcely beyond the foot of the shaft when they stumbled into a body of white damp and were stricken with death. The fire occurred on Monday. It was not until ten o'clock Tuesday morning that a sufficient ventilating current had been established to make it safe for men to descend. The greatest distance that it was possible to go from the foot of the shaft on Tuesday was seventy-five feet. Beyond that point the danger from suffocation was still imminent. Only three bodies had been thus far found.

Wednesday morning a rescuing party went up the plane at some distance from the foot of the shaft, and at the head of the plane they found a barrier across the gangway. It had been formed by placing a mine car in position and packing the space between it and the walls with clothing and refuse. This barrier was broken down, but there was no one behind it. Later another party was able to go a little farther, and came to a second barrier. Outside of this lay the dead body of John Bowen. He had come out for some purpose from behind the barricade, leaving open an aperture through which to crawl back, but before he could do so he had died from asphyxia. This barrier was broken down, and behind it lay the victims, one hundred and five of them, all dead, suffocated by the foul gases of the mine. The story of their experiences, their struggles, their sufferings, can never be known.

The disaster which occurred at the West Pittston mine on May 27, 1871, was similar in many respects to that at Avondale. In this case also the breaker, built over the shaft, the only opening to the mine, took fire and burned to the ground, closing the avenue of escape to thirty-six men and boys. These prisoners shut themselves into a chamber, building a barricade across the foot of it to keep out the foul gases; but when the rescuing party broke in to them on the following day fourteen of them were found dead and the rest were unconscious. Of those who were brought out alive four died soon after reaching the surface.

CHAPTER XIII.

THE ANTHRACITE COAL BREAKER.

IN the act of 1885 it is provided that "no inflammable structure other than a frame to sustain pulleys or sheaves shall be erected over the entrance of any opening connecting the surface with the underground workings of any mine, and no breaker or other inflammable structure for the preparation or storage of coal shall be erected nearer than two hundred feet to any such opening." This was for the purpose of preventing, if possible, such lamentable disasters as those of Avondale and West Pittston. The results of this legislation in providing greater security to the employees in mines is invaluable. Formerly it had been the custom to build not only the shaft-house over the opening into the mine, but the breaker itself, wherever there was one, was usually erected over the mouth of the shaft. This was convenient and economical, since the coal could be hoisted directly from the mine to the top of the breaker, without the delay of a horizontal transfer at the surface of the earth. Many of the shaft houses and breakers that had thus been built at the time of the passage of the act are still in

THE SLOAN COAL BREAKER, HYDE PARK, PA.

operation, and will so remain until the time of their utility is passed. But all new buildings are erected in accordance with the law.

At the mouth of the shaft heavy upright timbers are set up, inclosing the opening. These are united by cross-beams, and the whole structure is well braced. In this head-frame are set the sheaves, at a distance from the ground of from thirty to fifty feet, although, when the entire surface plant was under one cover, they were set much lower. These sheaves are huge upright wheels sixteen feet in diameter, over which the ropes pass that connect with the cages. A sheave similar in form to the bicycle wheel is now coming rapidly into use; it is found to bear a greater strain in comparison with its weight than does any other form.

The hoisting engine must be in the immediate vicinity of the shaft, and the rooms for this and the boiler, furnace, and pump are usually all under one roof. The iron or steel wire ropes extend from the sheaves in the head frame to the drum in the engine-room, around which they are coiled in such a manner that as one is being wound up the other is being unwound. Therefore as one carriage ascends the other descends by virtue of the same movement of the engine.

Since the breaker may receive coal from two or more openings it must be so located as to be convenient to both or all of them. If the ground slopes sufficiently the breaker may be so built that its head will be on a level with the head of the shaft. This will save breaker hoisting. When coal is brought out by a slope the track and grade of the slope are usually continued, by an open trestlework, from the mouth of the opening to the head of the breaker. Wherever it is possible to do so, the loaded cars are run by gravity from the mouth of the opening to the breaker, and the empty ones are drawn back by mules. Sometimes they are hauled both ways by mules, and sometimes a small steam locomotive engine is employed to draw them back and forth.

The coal breaker is an institution that is peculiar to the anthracite coal fields of Pennsylvania. Its need was made manifest early in the history of anthracite mining, its development was rapid, and it has now come to be wholly indispensable in the preparation of anthracite coal for the market. It is very seldom indeed that one sees this coal in the shape and size in which it was mined. All anthracite coal for domestic use is now broken, screened, and separated into grades of uniform size before being placed upon the market, and this work is done in the coal breakers.

Previous to the year 1844 these breakers were unknown. Several experiments had been made in the matter of breaking coal by machinery, but there had been no practical results, and the breaking still continued to be done by hand. In that year, however, a breaker after the modern plan was erected at the mines of Gideon Bast, in Schuylkill County, by J. & S. Battin of Philadelphia. It was started on the 28th of February, 1844. There were two cast-iron rollers in it, each about thirty inches long and thirty inches in diameter, and on the surface of these rollers were set iron teeth or projections about two and one half inches long and four inches from centre to centre. These rollers were placed horizontally, side by side, and were so geared that, as they revolved, their upper surfaces turned toward each other, and the teeth on one roller were opposite to the spaces on the other. These rolls were afterward improved by being perforated between the teeth, thus presenting less of solid surface to the coal, and causing less crushing. Another set of rollers was afterward added, being placed above the first set, and having the teeth larger and wider apart, so that large lumps of coal might first be broken into pieces small enough to be crushed readily by the lower set. After the perfecting of the rolls came the perfecting of the screens for the purpose of separating the broken coal into grades according to size. Before the introduction of coal breakers a hand screen was used. This screen was set in a frame, was cylindrical in form, and was slightly inclined from the horizontal. It was turned by a crank at one end, in the manner of a grindstone. The screen placed in the breaker was of much the same pattern, except that instead of being from five to eight feet long the length was increased to twenty feet, and the diameter correspondingly enlarged. Mr. Henry Jenkins of Pottsville then invented a method of weaving thick wire into screen plates about three feet wide, having the proper curve. These curved plates being joined together formed the necessary hollow cylinder. These separate plates are called jackets, and when one of them wears out it may be taken from the cylinder and replaced, with but little trouble and delay. The screen is set in heavy framework, and is inclined slightly from the horizontal. The first segment at the upper end of the screen is made of wire woven into a mesh so fine that only the smallest particles of coal will pass through it; the mesh of the next segment is larger, and that of the next larger still. The screen may contain from two to five segments in its length. Now the coal, being poured in on top of the revolving rolls, comes out from under them broken into small pieces, and passes immediately into the upper or highest end of the hollow cylindrical screen as it would pass into a barrel. But, as the screen revolves on its axis, the finer particles of coal fall out through the fine mesh of the first segment, and are carried away in an inclined trough, while the rest of the coal slides on to the next segment. Here the next smallest particles fall through and are carried away, and the process is continued until the lower end of the screen is reached, out of which end all the coal that was too large to pass through the mesh of the last segment is now poured. It will be seen that by this means the different sizes of coal have been separated from each other and can be carried by separate shutes to the loading place. This is the principle of the rolls and screens which are the main features of every coal breaker, though each breaker usually contains two or more sets of rolls and from eight to twelve screens. The Woodward breaker recently erected near Kingston, Pennsylvania, has six pairs of rollers and twenty screens. Some of these screens are double; that is, they have a larger outside screen surrounding the smaller one, and the coal that passes through the inner screen is caught by the outer one and again divided by means of a smaller mesh.

Before the days of breakers and screens coal was sent to market in the lump, as it came from the mine, and it was generally broken and prepared for use by the consumer. But when the separation of coal in the breaker became reduced to a system, the four smaller sizes than lump coal were soon graded. They were known as steamboat, egg, stove, and chestnut. It was thought at the time that no finer grade of coal than chestnut could be burned to advantage. But it was not long before a smaller size, known as pea coal, was separated, placed on the market, and readily sold;

and now, within recent years, another still smaller size called buckwheat has been saved from the refuse and has come into general use. Everything smaller than this is culm and goes to the waste pile. The names of the different sizes of marketable coal and the spaces over and through which they pass in the process of separation are given in the following table, taken from Saward's "Coal Trade Annual," for 1888 : —

		Over. Inches.	Through. Inches.
Lump coal	bars	$4\frac{1}{2}$ to 9	
Steamboat	"	$3\frac{1}{4}$ to 5	7
Broken	mesh	$2\frac{3}{8}$ to $2\frac{7}{8}$	$3\frac{1}{4}$ to $4\frac{1}{2}$
Egg	"	$1\frac{5}{8}$ to $2\frac{1}{4}$	$2\frac{3}{8}$ to $2\frac{7}{8}$
Large stove	"	$1\frac{1}{4}$ to $1\frac{5}{8}$	$1\frac{5}{8}$ to $2\frac{1}{4}$
Small stove	"	1 to $1\frac{1}{4}$	$1\frac{1}{4}$ to $1\frac{5}{8}$
Chestnut	"	$\frac{5}{8}$ to $\frac{3}{4}$	1 to $1\frac{1}{4}$
Pea	"	$\frac{3}{8}$ to $\frac{1}{2}$	$\frac{5}{8}$ to $\frac{7}{8}$
Buckwheat	"	$\frac{3}{16}$ to $\frac{3}{8}$	$\frac{3}{8}$ to $\frac{5}{8}$
Dirt	"		$\frac{3}{16}$ to $\frac{3}{8}$

The necessity which controls the form and construction of the breaker building is that the unbroken and unscreened coal must first be taken to a point in the building sufficiently high to allow of its passage, by gradual descent, with slow movement, through successive rolls, screens, shutes, and troughs until, thoroughly broken and fully cleaned and separated, it reaches the railroad cars, standing under the pockets, and is loaded into them for shipment. It is sometimes possible, as has already been intimated, to locate a breaker on the side of a hill so that the coal may be run into the head of it from the mine by a surface track without the necessity of hoisting. In this case the building will hug the hill, extending for a long distance down the slope of it, but without rising at any point to a great height from the surface of the ground. In these days, however, the breaker is more frequently erected in the valley. The general results are thought to be better, and the special convenience to railroad outlets to market is certainly greater. Besides this, the necessities of the case in shaft mining seem to demand it.

A peculiar and characteristic feature of a breaker so built is the great vertical height to which one portion of the building is run up. This is the portion that contains the shaft up which the coal is hoisted, and from the top of which it starts on its long descending route to the surface again. From one hundred to one hundred and fifty feet is not an unusual height for this portion of the building. From this topmost part of the structure the roof slopes down by stages, on one or two sides, widening out, running off at an angle to cover a wing, spreading by a projection here and there until, by the time the last ten feet in height are reached, the ground space covered by the building has come to be very great. Under the last or lowest portion of the structure are the railroad sidings on which the cars stand to be loaded from the many pockets in which the shutes have terminated. Two engines are necessary at the breaker, one a winding engine to hoist coal from the surface to the top of the breaker, and the other a breaker engine to move the rolls, screens, and other breaker machinery. The winding engine is usually put on the opposite side of the shaft tower from the rolls and screens, and the ropes from it, either exposed or under cover of a long sloping roof, reach up to the sheaves in the head frame. The breaker engine is usually housed in a wing at one side of the main building, while the several nests of boilers, under a separate cover, are required by the act of 1885 to be at least one hundred feet away from the breaker.

No one, having once seen and examined an anthracite coal breaker, could ever mistake one for a building erected for any other purpose. These breakers have a character peculiarly their own. They are the most prominent features in the landscape of every anthracite coal region, where they tower up black, majestic, many-winged, and many-windowed, in the range of almost every outlook.

When the mine car full of coal is hoisted to the head of the breaker it is run by two headmen from the carriage across the scale platform to the dump

THE ANTHRACITE COAL BREAKER. 185

shute bars on to which it is dumped. These are long, sloping, parallel iron bars, set two and one half inches apart. The dirt and all the coal that is small enough falls through these bars into a hopper, from which it is fed into a pair of screens, one on each side. These separate the dirt in the manner already described, and divide the clean coal into sizes smaller than, and including, egg. Each size as it falls through the segment of, or out at the end of, the screen, is caught in a separate shute and carried to a second set of revolving screens where it is again cleaned and separated, passing from these screens into the picking shutes. All the shutes or troughs in which the coal is carried have a sufficient inclination to make the material move by gravity, and, to decrease the amount of friction, the bottom and sides of each shute are lined with sheet iron. The large coals which passed over the dump shute bars now slide down to a second set of bars, set four and one half inches apart, called steamboat bars; all coal falling through these being separated by still a third set of bars into steamboat and egg, and eventually finding its way to the picking shutes or to the rolls which break the prepared coal. All coal which passed over the steamboat bars is lump coal, and, after having the slate and bony coal removed from it by hand as it passes, is carried into the lump-coal shute and sent down to the loading place; or else it is carried, by another shute, into the heavy rolls and crushed. As it emerges, broken, from these rolls, it passes into revolving screens, and the same process of screening and separating goes on that has been already described in the case of coal falling through the first or dump-shute bars. But all this broken, screened, and separated coal finds its way eventually into the picking shutes. These are narrow troughs down which the separate grades of coal pass slowly in shallow streams. Across the top of each trough, at two or more points in its route through the picking-room, narrow seats are placed on which boys sit facing up the shute. These boys are called slate pickers. It is their duty to pick out the pieces of slate, stone, or bone, from the stream of coal which passes under them, and throw this refuse into a trough at the side of the shute, from which point it slides rapidly away. The coal as it comes from the mine is full of waste material, so that the boy who sits first or highest on the shute has no trouble in finding plenty to do, and, work as hard as he may, much of the unfit material must still escape him. The boy who sits below him on the shute is able to give the passing stream a closer inspection and more careful treatment, and, should there be one still below, he must have sharp eyes and skillful fingers to detect worthless pieces that have been left by his comrades. The boys often put their feet in the shute and dam the coal back for a

SCREEN-ROOM IN BREAKER, SHOWING SCREEN AND SHUTES.

moment to give them time to throw out the abundance of slate that they may see, but no matter how careful they are, nor how many hands the coal may pass through in the picking process, a certain percentage of slate and bone is sure to remain. The slate pickers are not all stationed in one room, though the picking-room usually holds the greater number of them. They are put at the shutes in any part of the breaker where their services may be useful or necessary. Indeed, there are pickers who sit at the refuse shutes to pick out the pieces of good coal which have been inadvertently thrown in by the other pickers. In some breakers the coal passes from the shute across a gently sloping platform, by the side of which the boy sits to pick out the waste.

But the time is undoubtedly coming when the occupation of the picker boy will be gone. The inventive genius of the age has already devised machinery which does its work faster, better, and with greater certainty than the most conscientious breaker boy could hope to do it. The great collieries are, one by one, adopting the new methods, and the army of breaker boys is gradually but surely decreasing.

Nearly all the slate-picking machines are based on the fact that the specific gravity of coal is lighter than that of slate or stone. One method brings the principle of friction into play. A section, a few feet in length, of the floor of the shute down which the coal passes is made of stone. At the end of this stone section is a narrow slot cut in the floor, crosswise of the shute, and beyond the slot the iron bottom is continued as before. Now when the shallow stream of broken coal strikes the stone bottom the friction between that bottom and the pieces of slate and stone is so great that these particles are impeded in their progress, and by the time they reach the slot they have not impetus enough to cross it and must therefore drop into it and be carried away. But the friction between coal and stone is slight in comparison, and the pieces of coal retain enough of their impetus to carry them safely across the slot and on down the shute. This is not a perfect separation, and the coal and slate which it divides has usually to be looked over again, to insure satisfactory results. The best and most practicable invention thus far brought into use is that of Mr. Charles W. Ziegler, picker boss at the Von Storch colliery, Scranton. This machine acts somewhat upon the method last described, though by a system of rollers, levers, and screens in connection with it and attached to it, it is able to make quite perfect separation of the coal and slate. Two or three of these machines placed on a single shute should do the work required of them very thoroughly.

The experience of domestic buyers of coal would seem to indicate, either that the picker boys do not do their whole duty or that the picking machines have not yet been made perfect. But it must be remembered that the separation of slate and bony coal from good material is made only in a rough and general way in the mine, and that a very large percentage of the output, as it reaches the breaker, is unfit for use. To clean and separate this material thoroughly, therefore, requires much labor, and extreme care and skill.

After these separate streams of coal have passed the scrutiny of the picker boys or the test of the picking machine, the shutes in which they run are narrowed into pockets or bins, closed at the end by a gate. The pocket projects over the car track high enough from it for a railroad coal car to stand beneath, and the coal is then fed from the pocket into the car at will.

There is also a loading place for the rock and slate which have been separated from the coal on its way through the breaker; and there are two or three points where the coal dirt is gathered from its pockets to be taken away. All this refuse is run out by separate tracks to a convenient distance from the breaker and there dumped.

It is estimated that sixteen per cent. of the material which goes into the breaker to be prepared comes out as waste, and is sent to the refuse dump. It can readily be supposed, therefore, that in the course of a few years these waste heaps will grow to an enormous size; and as a matter of fact they do. The dirt or culm, which includes all material finer than buckwheat coal, is usually dumped on a separate pile from the rock, slate, and bony coal, since it is not wholly without at least prospective value. It has been used frequently in the coal regions to fill in beneath railroad tracks supported by trestle-work, and it is valuable as a foundation on which to lay stone flagging for footwalks, since it does not yield readily to the action of frost. Culm has also been utilized by adding to it a certain percentage of mucilaginous or pitchy material and compressing it into bricks for fuel. In some European countries a large amount of waste is burned in this way, but in America the cost of preparation is still too great to permit of competition with prepared anthracite. The most characteristic feature of scenery in the anthracite coal regions, aside from the breakers themselves, is the presence of these great, bare, black hills of culm, shining in the sunlight, smoothly white under the snows of winter. Sometimes these culm banks take fire, either spontaneously or as the result of carelessness or accident. If the pile is near enough to the breaker to menace it, or near enough to an outcrop to carry combustion into the coal of the mine, the fire must be extinguished, and this is sometimes done with much labor and at great expense. If no danger is apprehended, the fire is allowed to smoulder until it burns out, a process which may take months or even years, during which time little blue flames flicker on the surface of the bank, the sky above it is tinged with red at night, and the whole black hillside is finally covered with great blotches of white ash. To the poor people who live in the vicinity of the breakers these heaps of refuse coal are an unmixed blessing. Pieces of good coal are always being thrown out inadvertently with the waste, and the bony coal that is discarded is not by any means without value as a fuel; indeed it makes a very respectable fire. So, too, one can obtain, with a screen, from the culm heap quite a little percentage of material that will burn. Thus it comes about that every day women and children and old men go to these black hills with hammer and screen and gather fuel for their fires, and carry it home in bags, or wheelbarrows, or little handcarts. It is the old story over again of the gleaners in the field.

CHAPTER XIV.

IN THE BITUMINOUS COAL MINES.

A BRIEF history of the discovery and introduction into use of the bituminous coals of Pennsylvania has already been given; but only casual reference has been made to the methods of mining in the bituminous regions. It is true that of the one hundred and twenty thousand square miles of workable coal beds in the United States less than five hundred square miles are of anthracite coal. It is true, also, that more than two thirds of the coal produced in the United States during the year 1887 was of the bituminous variety, and that the income from bituminous coal during that year was nearly twice as much as the income from anthracite. Yet it is obvious that in any description of coal mining methods the anthracite mines should be used as the chief examples. This is not only because of the greater commercial importance of anthracite, and of its greater familiarity as a domestic fuel, but it is principally because of the far greater skill, judgment, and ingenuity required in mining it and preparing it for market. In the bituminous regions the coal is soft, lies flat and near the surface, and is mined by the simplest methods. The reader is already familiar with some of the complications, obstacles, and problems that meet and beset the operator in the anthracite regions, and with the great labor, vast expenditures, and high degree of skill necessary to reach, take out, and prepare the anthracite coal. In view of these facts no excuse is necessary for attaching the greater importance to the description of methods in the anthracite region. But a brief outline of the systems in vogue at the bituminous mines will not be uninteresting, so far at least as they differ from those in use at the anthracite mines.

In the year 1887 a little more than one third of the bituminous coal output of the United States came from the Pennsylvania mines. Pittsburgh is the centre of the soft coal trade of that state, and the principal coal seam of the region is known as the "Pittsburgh bed." It is included in an area about fifty miles square, and varies in thickness from two or three feet in the northwestern part, and six feet at Pittsburgh, to ten feet up the Monongahela River, and twelve feet up the Youghiogeny. The exhaustion of so vast a coal bed is a practical impossibility, and the questions that engage the attention of the mining engineer in these regions are not so much questions of the economy of coal as they are questions of the economy of labor. The coal lies near the surface, and the outcrops on the flanks of the hills and banks of the rivers are so numerous that most of the mining can be, and is, done by drift above water level. The outlay of capital required in opening a mine is therefore very small, marketable coal being obtained at almost the first blow of the pick.

Before mining operations are begun a complete survey is made of all outcroppings, and their differences in level are obtained. From this data a comparatively accurate knowledge may be had of the position of the coal bed under ground, as the dip of the seams is very moderate and uniform, and but few faults and other irregularities are encountered. It is then decided where to locate the mouth of the drift so that the entry can be driven in on the rise of the coal and the mine become self-draining. It is important, however, to have the opening at a convenient point near the river or railroad, and it is usually so made if possible, even though the dip should be away from the opening. The inclination is always so slight as not to interfere greatly with the hauling of cars, and it is not much of a task to make a separate opening for drainage. The coal seam is divided by vertical cleavage planes, running at right angles to each other, one of which is known as the *butt* cleavage and the other as the *face* cleavage. The main entries are driven in, if possible, on the face cleavage, as are also the chambers, or "rooms" as they are called here; while the entries from which the rooms are turned are always driven on the butt cleavage. The drift, or main entry, has an airway running parallel with it; sometimes it has one on each side of it. It is driven eight or nine feet in width, except where two tracks are necessary, in which case it is made from twelve to fifteen feet wide. These double or treble entries are parallel to each other, and are separated by a wall of coal from twenty-five to forty feet in width. Through this wall, at about every thirty yards, entrances, or, as they are called here, "break-throughs," are made, having the same width as the entry. The height of roof in the entries of the Pittsburgh seam is usually five and one half or six feet in the clear. At right angles to the main entry butt entries are driven in pairs, parallel to each other and about thirty or forty feet apart, with break-throughs or cross-cuts for the passage of air, as on the main entries. From each of these butt entries, at right angles to them, and in opposite directions, the rooms are driven. They are made about twenty-one feet wide, with pillars between them twelve feet thick, and are not often more than eighty yards in length. They are usually driven to meet the faces of the rooms which are being worked from the next parallel butt entry, or are extended to that butt entry itself. At the point where the room turns off from the butt entry it is made only seven feet wide for a distance of from fifteen to twenty-one feet, then the room is widened out to its full width of twenty-one feet. The track on which the mine wagon runs is laid straight up the side of the room from the opening at the entry, occupying a clear space about seven feet wide. The rest of the room is well filled with the refuse which has been separated from the coal as mining has progressed, and the roof is supported by an abundance of props, or "posts" as they are here called. In one room, with an ordinary roof, about six hundred and fifteen posts would be necessary. The pillars are long, the distances between breakthroughs averaging thirty yards. This is known as the "double entry" system, to distinguish it from the single entry system which was formerly in general use. The method by single entry consisted in driving the butt entries singly, about one hundred and sixty yards apart, and the face entries the same distance apart, at right angles to the butt entries, thus laying off the mine in large square blocks which were then mined out. The difficulty with this system was that from twenty-five to fifty per cent. of the pillars were necessarily lost, while by the double entry system, which now prevails, all or nearly all the pillars can be taken out.

Of course the features in the plan of each mine vary according to the special necessities of that mine, but in general they do not differ greatly from those that have been described.

The method of cutting coal here is also peculiar to the soft coal mines. The miner has a pick with

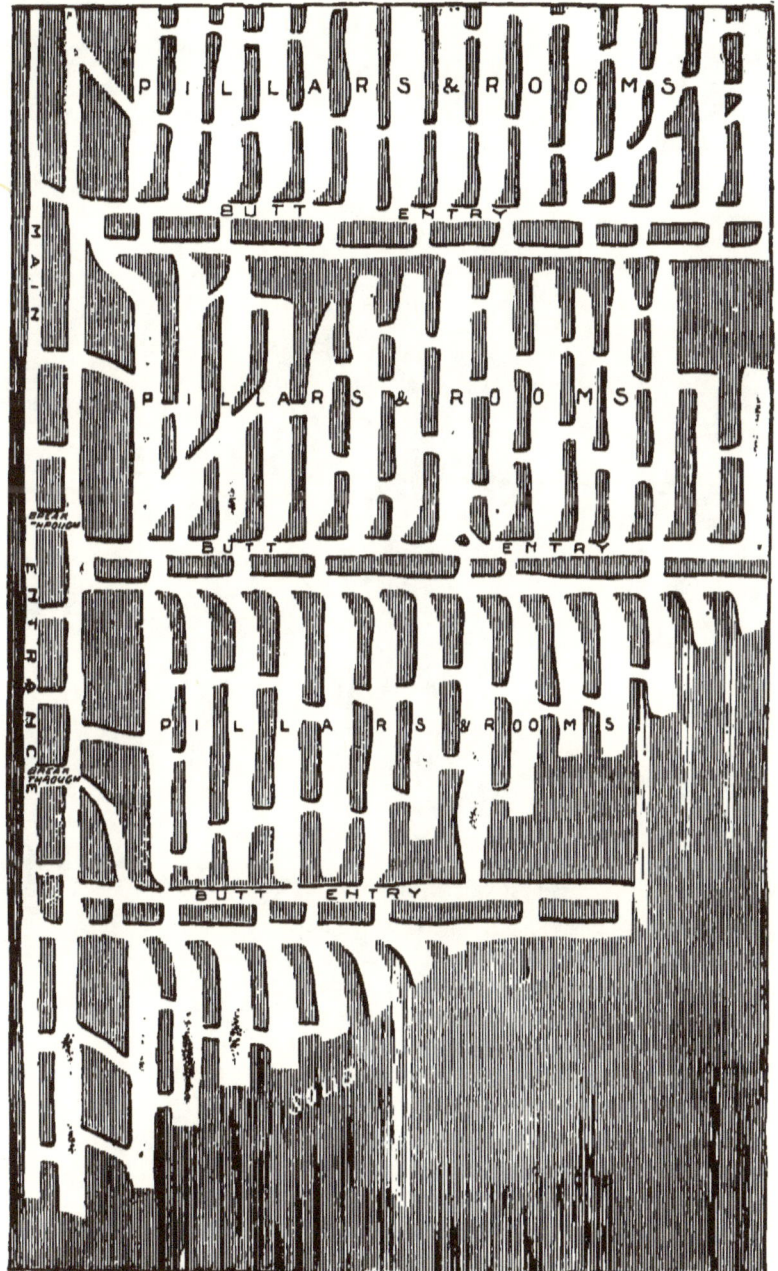

PLAN OF A BITUMINOUS COAL MINE.

sharp, pointed ends, and with this he cuts a horizontal groove or channel, from two and a half to three and a half feet deep across the entire width of the entry or room. This groove is cut in that horizontal section of the face known as the bearing-in section. It may be in the bottom layer of coal, or it may be one or two feet above the bottom. The process itself is known as "bearing in," "under cutting," "holing," or "undermining." While he is at this work the miner must lie on the floor of the room, partly on his side, but with hands and arms free. When the horizontal groove has been completed a vertical groove similar to it in size and shape is made at one side of the face. These channels are sometimes cut with mining machines having compressed air for a motive power. This machine is small but powerful. It is placed on a low inclined platform at the face of coal, and is operated by a man called a "runner." The inclination of the platform causes the machine, which is on wheels, to gravitate constantly toward, and to press against, the face of coal. The compressed air cylinder drives a piston-rod to which is attached a steel bit two inches in diameter projecting from the front of the machine. This bit strikes the coal with sharp, swift blows, chipping it out in small fragments, and eats its way rapidly into the seam. The compressed air is carried to the machine in an iron pipe from the compressing engine, which is located at the mouth of the mine.

When a machine is used, seven men usually work three rooms. Three of these men are contractors or partners, three of them are laborers employed by the contractors, and one of them, called the "scraper," is a laborer employed by the coal company. When the channel has been cut a sufficient depth and distance the coal above it is brought down either by wedging or blasting. If blasting is to be resorted to it will be unnecessary to cut the vertical groove. If the bearing-in channel was cut above the floor, the bottom coal is then lifted by wedging, and broken up. The miners do the cutting and blasting, the laborers break up the coal and load it into the mine wagons, and the scraper is kept busy cleaning the cuttings away from the channels and attending to the lamps.

The mine car track that is extended up into the room is of wooden rails, and the empty wagon is pushed in to the face by the laborers, and loaded and run out by them to the entry. Each wagon will hold a little more than a ton, and a mule will draw four wagons to the mouth of the drift. The wheels of the mine car are set close to each other, near the middle of the car, to facilitate its movement around sharp curves; the doors at the ends of the car are swung from a bar hinge at the top, and the cars are dumped in the same manner as those in the anthracite region. In some of the bituminous mines a small locomotive is used to draw the trains of mine wagons from the working parts of the mine to the opening. It will draw from twelve to sixteen wagons at a time, and will do the work of twenty mules. There is usually a separate split of the air current to supply the locomotive road in order to keep the smoke out of the working rooms.

When a set of rooms has been driven to its limit the miners then "draw back the rib;" that is, take out the pillars between the rooms, beginning at the face and working back. Posts must be used freely to support the roof while this work is in progress, about sixty or seventy being necessary in drawing a rib.

Ventilation here is obtained by both the fan and the furnace systems. In mines that are worked below water level fire damp often accumulates, but where the coal does not descend at any point below the water-level line, there is no probability that mine gases will be found.

As has already been said, the usual method of entry into the bituminous mines has been, and still is, by drift. But as the working faces of the mines recede farther and farther from the general lines of outcrop, it often becomes necessary to resort to the method of entry by shaft, and this latter method will doubtless in time supersede the former almost entirely. The main shaft, as it is now constructed, is usually about twenty feet long by nine feet wide, and has three compartments, two for hoisting and one for ventilation and pumping. It rarely exceeds two hundred feet in depth. The hoisting apparatus is much like that in use in the anthracite districts. Air shafts from fifty to one hundred feet deep, sunk for purposes of ventilation and drainage, are frequent, and stair shafts in which are fixed ladders for the purpose of ascent and descent, and which may be used as air shafts also, are not uncommon. Slopes, like those in the anthracite regions, are not usual here; the coal seams do not dip sufficiently to make them practicable. Narrow rock slopes are sometimes driven diagonally through the strata, at an inclination of twenty degrees or less, to strike the coal bed, but they are used only as air ways, as traveling ways for men and mules, and to serve as the "second opening" required by the mine law.

In the bituminous regions coal breakers are unnecessary and are unknown. As the vertical planes of cleavage of the coal are at right angles to each other, and as the stratification is nearly horizontal, the coal when broken takes a cubical form, large blocks of it being made up of smaller cubes, and these of still smaller, to an almost microscopic limit. All slate is separated from the coal as it is mined, and the refuse is piled up in the room.

The mine wagon is loaded only with good coal, and is taken directly from the mine to a building which, with its appliances, is called a "tipple." It is here dumped into a screen, it runs from the screen into a car or boat, and is then ready to be hauled or floated to market.

If the opening of the mine is practically on the same level as the tipple the arrangements are very simple, as no extra motive power is required to get the cars to the dumping place. It is usual, however, to find the opening at a higher point than the tipple, since the latter must always be at the railroad track or on the bank of a river. It becomes necessary, therefore, in this case, to raise and lower the cars between the opening of the mine and the tipple. This is usually done by the inclined plane system, in which the loaded cars descending draw the light ones up. The same system is much used in the anthracite mines, and has already been explained.

The railroad tipple consists simply of a frame building from forty to sixty feet long, fifteen feet high, and from eighteen to thirty feet wide. This structure is set upon four or five plain timber bents, and its floor is usually twenty-seven feet higher than the top of the track rails which run beneath the outer end of it. A platform on this floor is so adjusted by a single shaft that, when a loaded car is pushed on it, it tips forward to an angle of about thirty degrees. The end gate of the wagon is then opened and the coal runs out on to the screen. This screen is simply a set of longitudinal iron bars inclined outwardly at distances apart of one and one half inches. All coal that passes over these bars is called "lump coal" and is run into a sheet-iron pan suspended from the scales platform, where it is weighed, and it is then dropped directly into a car standing on the track below it. The coal which passed through the first set of bars has, in the mean time, fallen on to a second screen with bars only three quarters of an inch apart. The coal that passes over these bars is called nut coal, and is also weighed and dropped into the cars, while the coal that passes through the bars is called "slack." This is dropped into a shute, is carried by it into a car on the slack track, and is run thence to the dumping ground. When all three kinds of coal are loaded together it is called "run of mine," while lump and nut coal together make "three quarter coal." These tipples may, of course, be built with two sets of screens and platforms, and thus be made to do double work, and some of them are so built. Under the projecting end of the tipple there are usually four tracks; the first or outside one for box-cars, the next for lump-coal cars, the next for nut-coal cars, and the last for cars for slack. Four men operate a single railroad tipple; two dump and weigh the coal above, while the others trim and move the railroad cars on the track below. To this number a helper is often added, both above and below. Besides these men a boy is usually employed to rake the nut coal from the lower screening bars where it sticks and prevents the slack from passing through. Sometimes it takes two boys to do this work properly. Boys are also employed to push the slack with a scraper down the shutes into the car on the slack track when the elevation of the tipple above the rails is not sufficient to afford the necessary grade. Bars are being largely superseded now by revolving screens for separating slack from nut coal; they do the work far better, and make the employment of a raking boy unnecessary.

The river tipple is operated in much the same way as the railroad tipple, except that its apparatus must be so arranged as to accommodate itself to high or low water. The floor of the river tipple is usually placed from forty to fifty feet above low-water mark, and the weighing pan is held in position by a counter-weight, which may be raised or lowered at pleasure. A small stationary engine, or a hand windlass, draws the empty boat or barge into position under that end of the tipple which projects over the water. About twice as many men are required to operate a river tipple as are necessary to operate a railroad tipple, and while the railroad tipple costs but from two thousand to four thousand dollars the river tipple is built at an expense of from four thousand to ten thousand dollars. But even this latter figure is small when compared with the cost of an anthracite breaker, which may run anywhere from twenty thousand to one hundred thousand dollars.

CHAPTER XV.

THE BOY WORKERS AT THE MINES.

In the coal mines of the United States boys are employed at two kinds of labor: to attend the doors on the traveling roads, and to drive the mules. This is known as inside work. Their outside work consists in picking slate at the breaker, and in driving the mules that draw mine cars on the surface. No one of these different kinds of employment is such as to overtax the physical strength of boys of a proper age, but they are all confining, some are dangerous, and some are laborious. Yet the system of child labor in the coal mines of America has never been comparable to that which was formerly in vogue in Great Britain. The British "Coal Mines Regulation Act" of 1872 remedied the then existing evils to a considerable extent; but the hardships still to be endured by children in the British mines are greater than those which their American brothers must suffer. The act of 1872, just referred to, provides that boys under ten years of age shall not be employed under ground, and that boys between ten and twelve years of age shall be allowed to work only in thin mines. It is the duty of these

THE BOY WORKERS AT THE MINES.

children to push the cars, or trams as they are called, from the working faces to the main road and back. Boys who are thus employed are called "hurriers" or "putters." They are often obliged to crawl on their hands and knees, pushing the car ahead of them, because the roof of the excavation is so low. That is why boys who are so young are allowed to work here; because, being small, they can the more readily crawl through the passages cut in these thin seams, which often do not have a vertical measurement of more than from twenty to twenty-eight inches. The act of 1872 forbids the employment of females in the British mines; but formerly not only boys but girls and women also worked underground. There was then no restriction as to age, and girls were sent into the mines to labor at an earlier age than were boys, because they were credited with being smarter and more obedient. It was common to find children of both sexes not more than six years old working underground; and girls of five years were employed at the same tasks as boys of six or eight. They took the coal from the working faces in the thin mines to the foot of the pit. Sometimes they carried it, sometimes they drew it in little carts. The older children and young women had a sort of sledge, called a "corve," on which they dragged the coal, but sometimes they preferred to carry it in baskets on their backs. They were called "pannier women." The girls tucked their hair up under their caps, dressed like their brothers, and in the darkness of the mine could scarcely be distinguished from boys. And the girls and boys not only dressed alike, but worked alike, lived alike, and were treated alike at their tasks, and that treatment was rough and harsh at the very best. As the girls grew they were given harder work to do. On one occasion Mr. William Hunter, the mine foreman at Ormiston Colliery said that in the mines women always did the lifting or heavy part of the work, and that neither they nor the children were treated like human beings. "Females," he said, "submit to work in places in which no man nor lad could be got to labor. They work on bad roads, up to their knees in water, and bent nearly double. The consequence of this is that they are attacked with disease, drag out a miserable existence, or are brought prematurely to the grave." Says Robert Bold, the eminent miner: "In surveying the workings of an extensive colliery underground a married woman came forward, groaning under an excessive weight of coals, trembling in every nerve, and almost unable to keep her knees from sinking under her. On coming up she said in a plaintive, melancholy voice: 'Oh, sir! this is sore, sore, sore work. I would to God that the first woman who tried to bear coals had broken her back and none ever tried it again.'"

One cannot read of such things as these, of a

slavery that condemned even the babes to a life of wretched toil in the blackness of the mines, and then wonder that the great heart of Mrs. Browning should have been wrenched by the contemplation of such sorrow until she gave voice to her feeling in that most pathetic and wonderful of all her poems, "The Cry of the Children."

"Do ye hear the children weeping, O my brothers!
   Ere the sorrow comes with years?
They are leaning their young heads against their mothers,
   And *that* cannot stop their tears.
The young lambs are bleating in the meadows,
   The young birds are chirping in their nest,
The young fawns are playing with the shadows,
   The young flowers are blooming toward the west.
But the young, young children, O my brothers!
   They are weeping bitterly;
They are weeping in the playtime of the others,
   In the country of the free.

"'For, oh!' say the children, 'we are weary,
   And we cannot run or leap;
If we cared for any meadows, it were merely
   To drop down in them and sleep.
Our knees tremble sorely in the stooping,
   We fall upon our faces trying to go,
And, underneath our heavy eyelids drooping,
   The reddest flower would look as pale as snow.
For all day we drag our burden tiring,
   Through the coal dark underground,
Or all day we drive the wheels of iron
   In the factories round and round.'

"'How long,' they say, 'how long, O cruel nation!
   Will you stand to move the world on a child's heart,
Stifle down, with a mailed heel, its palpitation,
   And tread onward to your throne amid the mart?

> Our blood splashes upward, O gold heaper!
> And your purple shows your path;
> But the child's sob in the silence curses deeper
> Than the strong man in his wrath.'"

In the United States neither girls nor women have ever been employed in or about the mines. The legislative prohibition of such employment, enacted in Pennsylvania in 1885, was therefore unnecessary but not inappropriate.

The general mine law of Pennsylvania of 1870, which was the first to limit the employment of boys in the mines according to their age, fixed twelve years as the age under which a boy might not work underground; but maintained silence as to the age at which he might work at a colliery outside. This provision was amended and enlarged by the act of 1885, which prohibited the employment of boys under fourteen years of age inside the mines, and of boys under twelve years of age in or about the outside structures or workings of a colliery.

The duties of a driver boy are more laborious than those of a door-tender, but less monotonous and tiresome than those of a slate picker or breaker-boy. When the mules are kept in the mines night and day, as they frequently are in deep workings, the driver must go down the shaft before seven o'clock, get his mule from the mine stable, bring him to the foot of the shaft, and hitch him to a trip of empty cars. He usually takes in to the working faces four empty cars and brings out four loaded ones. When he is ready to start in with his trip, he climbs into the forward car, cracks his whip about the beast's head, and goes off shouting. His whip is a long, braided leather lash, attached to a short stout stick for a handle. He may have a journey of a mile or more before reaching the foot of the first chamber he is to supply; but when he comes to it he unfastens the first car from the others and drives the mule up the chamber with it, leaving it at a convenient distance from the face. He continues this process at each of the chambers in succession, until his supply of empty cars is exhausted. At the foot of the last chamber which he visits he finds a loaded car to which he attaches his mule, and picking up other loaded cars on his way back, he makes up his return trip, and is soon on the long, unbroken journey to the shaft. There are sidings at intervals along the heading, where trips going in the opposite direction are met and passed, and where there is opportunity to stop for a moment and talk with or chaff some other driver boy. If there be a plane on the main road, either ascending or descending from the first level, two sets of driver boys and mules are necessary, one set to draw cars between the breasts and the plane, and the other set to draw them between the plane and the shaft. Of course, in steep pitching seams, all cars are left at the foot of the chamber and are loaded there. There are two dangers to which driver boys are chiefly subjected; one is that of being crushed between cars, or between cars and pillars or props, and the other is that of being kicked or bitten by vicious mules. The boy must not only learn to drive, but he must learn to govern his beast and keep out of harm's way. He is generally sufficiently skillful and agile to do this, but it is not unusual to read of severe injuries to boys, given by kicking, bucking, or biting mules.

If the mine in which the boy works is entered by drift or tunnel, his duties lie partly outside of it, since he must bring every trip of cars not only to the mouth of the opening but to the breaker or other dumping place, which may be located at a considerable distance from the entrance to the mine. So that for a greater or less number of times each day he has from ten minutes to half an hour in the open air. In the summer time, when the weather is pleasant, this occasional glimpse of out-of-doors is very gratifying to him. He likes to be in the sunlight, to look out over the woods and fields, to feel the fresh wind blowing in his face, and to breathe an unpolluted atmosphere. But in the winter time, when it is cold, when the storms are raging, when the snow and sleet are whirled savagely into his face, then the outside portion of his trip is not pleasant. In the mine he finds a uniform temperature of about sixty degrees Fahrenheit. To go from this, within ten minutes, without additional clothing, into an atmosphere in which the mercury stands at zero, and where the wind is blowing a hurricane, is necessarily to suffer. It cannot be otherwise. So there is no lagging outside on winter days; the driver boy delivers his loads, gets his empty cars, and hastens back to the friendly shelter of the mine. At such openings as these the mine stable is outside, and the boy must go there in the morning to get his mule, and must leave him there when he quits work at night. Sometimes, when the mining is done by shaft or slope, there is a separate entrance for men and mules, a narrow tunnel or slope, not too steep, and in this case, though his duties lie entirely in the mine, the driver boy must take the mule in from the outside stable in the morning and bring him back at night.

One afternoon I chanced to be in a certain mine in the Wyoming district, in company with the fire boss. We were standing in a passage that led to one of these mule ways. In the distance we heard a clattering of hoofs, growing louder as it came nearer, and, as we stepped aside, a mule went dashing by with a boy lying close on his back, the flame from the little lamp in the boy's cap just a tiny backward streak of blue that gave no light. They had appeared from the intense darkness and had disappeared into it again almost while one could draw a breath. I looked at the fire boss inquiringly.

"Oh! that's all right," he said, "they've got

through work and they're going out, and the mule is in just as much of a hurry as the boy is."

"But the danger," I suggested, "of racing at such speed through narrow, winding passages, in almost total darkness!"

"Oh!" he replied, "that beast knows the way out just as well as I do, and he can find it as easy as if he could see every inch of it, and I don't know but what he can. Anyway the boy ain't afraid if the mule ain't."

In deep mines, as has already been said, it is customary to build stables not far from the foot of the shaft, and to keep the mules there except when for any reason there is a long suspension of work. At many mines, however, the greater convenience of having the stables on the surface induces the operators to have the mules hoisted from the shaft every night and taken down every morning. They step on the carriage very demurely, and ascend or descend without making trouble. They are especially glad to go up to their stables at night. Where mules are fed in the mine, and especially in those mines that have stables in them, rats are usually found. How they get down a shaft is a mystery. The common explanation is that they go with the hay. But they take up their quarters in the mine, live, thrive, increase rapidly, and grow to an enormous size. They are much like the wharf rats that infest the wharves of great cities, both in size and ugliness. They are very bold and aggressive, and when attacked will turn on their enemy, whether man or beast, and fight to the death. There is a superstition among miners to the effect that when the rats leave a mine some great disaster is about to take place in it; probably an extensive fall. Rats are hardly to be credited, however, with an instinct that would lead them to forecast such an event with more certainty than human experience and skill can do.

But it is not improbable that the driver boy and his mule will be superseded, at no distant day, by electricity. In one instance at least this new motive power has already been put into use. This is at the Lykens Valley Colliery of the Lykens Valley Coal Company, in Dauphin County, Pennsylvania.

The duty of an outside driver boy is to take the loaded cars from the head of the shaft or slope to the breaker, and to bring the empty ones back; his work being all done in the open air. Of late this service, especially where the distance is considerable, is performed by a small locomotive, which draws trains of as many cars as can well be held together. The wages paid to inside driver boys by the Pennsylvania Coal Company in 1888 were from one dollar to one dollar and ten cents a day, and to outside driver boys eighty-eight cents a day.

The door boys are usually younger and smaller

than the driver boys, and though their duty is not so laborious as that of the latter class, it is far more monotonous and tiresome. The door boy must be at his post when the first trip goes in in the morning, and must remain there till the last one comes out at night. He is alone all day, save when other boys and men pass back and forth through his door, and he has but little opportunity for companionship. He fashions for himself a rude bench to sit on; sometimes he has a rope or other contrivance attached to his door by which he can open it without rising; but usually he is glad to move about a little to break the monotony of his task. There is little he can do to entertain himself, except perhaps to whittle. He seldom tries to read; indeed, the light given forth by a miner's lamp is too feeble to read by. In rare cases the door boy extinguishes his light, on the score of economy, and sits in darkness, performing his duties by the light of the lamps of those who pass. But there are few who can endure this. It is hard enough to bear the oppressive silence that settles down on the neighborhood when no cars are passing; if darkness be added to this the strain becomes too great, the effect too depressing, a child cannot bear it. The wages of the door boy are about sixty-five cents per day.

Although the duties of the breaker boy or slate picker are more laborious and more monotonous than those of either driver boy or door tender, he does not receive so high a rate of wages as either of them. His daily compensation is only from fifty to sixty-five cents, and he works ten hours a day. At seven o'clock in the morning he must have climbed the dark and dusty stairway to the screen room, and taken his place on the little bench across the long shute. The whistle screams, the ponderous machinery is set in motion, the iron-teethed rollers begin to revolve heavily, crunching the big lumps of coal as they turn, the deafening noise breaks forth, and then the black, shallow streams of broken coal start on their journey down the iron-sheathed shutes, to be screened and cleaned, and picked and loaded.

At first glance it would not seem to be a difficult task to pick slate, but there are several things to be taken into consideration before a judgment can properly be made up in the matter. To begin with, the work is confining and monotonous. The boy must sit on his bench all day, bending over constantly to look down at the coal that is passing beneath him. His tender hands must become toughened by long and harsh contact with sharp pieces of slate and coal, and after many cuts and bruises have left marks and scars on them for a lifetime. He must breathe an atmosphere thick with the dust of coal, so thick that one can barely see across the screen room when the boys are sitting at their tasks. It is no wonder that a person long subjected to the irritating presence of this dust in his bronchial tubes and on his lungs is liable to suffer from the disease known as "miner's consumption." In the hot days of summer the screen-room is a stifling place. The sun pours its rays upon the broad, sloping roof of the breaker, just overhead; the dust-laden atmosphere is never cleared or freshened by so much as a breath of pure sweet air, and the very thought of green fields and blossoming flowers and the swaying branches of trees renders the task here to be performed more burdensome. Yet even this is not so bad as it is to work here in the cold days of winter. It is almost impossible to heat satisfactorily by any ordinary method so rambling a structure as a breaker necessarily is, and it is quite impossible to divide the portion devoted to screening and picking into closed rooms. The screen-rooms are, therefore, always cold. Stoves are often set up in them, but they radiate heat through only a limited space, and cannot be said to make the room warm. Notwithstanding the presence of stoves, the boys on the benches shiver at their tasks, and pick slate with numb fingers, and suffer from the extreme cold through many a winter day. But science and the progress of ideas are coming to their aid. In some breakers, recently erected, steam-heating pipes have been introduced into the screen-rooms with great success; the warmth and comfort given by them to the little workers is beyond measurement. Fans have been put into the breakers, also,

SLATE PICKERS AT WORK.

to collect and carry away the dust and keep the air of the picking-room clean and fresh, and electric lamps have been swung from the beams to be lighted in the early mornings and late afternoons, that the young toilers may see to do their work. Indeed, such improvements as these pass beyond the domain of science and progress into that of humanitarianism.

When night comes no laborer is more rejoiced at leaving his task than is the breaker boy. One can see his eyes shine and his white teeth gleam as he starts out into the open air, while all else, hands, face, clothing, are thickly covered with coal dust, are black and unrecognizable. But he is happy because his day's work is done and he is free, for a few hours at least, from the tyranny of the "cracker boss." For, in the estimation of the picker boys, the cracker boss is indeed the most tyrannical of masters. How else could they regard a man whose sole duty it is to be constantly in their midst, to keep them at their tasks, to urge them to greater zeal and care, to repress all boyish freaks, to rule over them almost literally with a rod of iron? But, alas! the best commentary on the severity of his government is that it is necessary.

As has already been said, the day is evidently not far distant when the work which the breaker boy now does will be performed almost wholly by machinery. And this will be not alone because the machine does its work better, more surely, more economically, than the breaker boy has done his, but it will be also because the requisite number of boys for breaker work will not be obtainable. Even now it is more than difficult to keep the ranks of the slate pickers full. · Parents in the coal regions of to-day have too much regard for the health, the comfort, the future welfare of their children, to send them generally to such grinding tasks as these. This is one of the signs of that advancing civilization which has already lifted girls and women from this, for them, exhausting and degrading labor at the collieries; which is lessening, one by one, the hardships of the boys who still toil there; which, it is fondly hoped, will in the course of time give to all children the quiet of the school-room, the freedom of the play-ground, and the task that love sets, in place of that irksome toil that stunts the body and dwarfs the soul. It is now mainly from the homes of the very poor that the child-workers at the collieries are recruited, and the scant wages that they earn may serve to keep bread in the mouths of the younger children of their households and clothing on their own backs.

Accidents to boys employed at the mines are of frequent occurrence. Scarcely a day passes but the tender flesh of some poor little fellow is cut or bruised, or his bones twisted and broken. It is only the more serious of these accidents that reach the notice of the mine inspector and are returned in his annual report. Yet, to the humanitarian and the lover of children, these annual returns tell a sad story. The mine inspector's reports for 1887 show that in the anthracite region alone during that year eighteen boys fifteen years of age and under were killed while fulfilling the duties of their employment in and about the coal mines, and that seventy-three others were seriously injured, many of them doubtless maimed for life. These figures tell their own story of sorrow and of suffering.

Yet with all their hardships it cannot be said that the boys who work in the collieries are wholly unhappy. It is difficult, indeed, to so limit, confine, and gird down a boy that he will not snatch some enjoyment from his life; and these boys seek to get much.

One who has been long accustomed to them can generally tell the nature of their several occupations by the way in which they try to amuse themselves. The driver boys are inclined to be rude and boisterous in their fun, free and impertinent in their manner, and chafe greatly under restraint. The slate pickers, confined all day at their tasks, with no opportunity for sport of any kind, are inclined to bubble over when night and freedom come, but, as a rule, they are too tired to display more than a passing effort at jocularity. Door boys are quiet and contemplative. Sitting so long alone in the darkness they become thoughtful, sober, sometimes melancholy. They go silently to their homes when they leave the mine; they do not stop to play tricks or to joke with their fellows; they do not run, nor sing, nor whistle. Darkness and silence are always depressing, and so much of it in these young lives cannot help but sadden without sweetening them. We shall never see, in America, those horrors of child slavery that drew so passionate a protest from the great-hearted Mrs. Browning, but certainly, looking at the progress already made, it is not too much to hope for that the day will come when no child's hand shall ever again be soiled by the labor of the mine.

It will be a fitting close to this chapter, and will be an act of justice to the memory of a brave and heroic boy, to relate the story of Martin Crahan's sacrifice at the time of the disaster at the West Pittston shaft. Martin was a driver boy, of humble parentage, poor and unlearned. He was in the mine when the fire in the breaker broke out, and he ran, with others, to the foot of the shaft. But just as he was about to step on the carriage that would have taken him in safety to the surface he bethought him of the men on the other side of the shaft, who might not have heard of the fire, and his brave heart prompted him to go to them with the alarm. He asked another boy to go with him, but that boy refused. He did not stop to parley; he started at once alone. But while he ran through the dark passage on his errand of mercy, the carriage went speeding, for the last time, up the burning shaft. He gave the alarm and returned, in breathless haste, with those whom he had sought; but it was too late, the cage had already fallen. When the party was driven away from the foot of the shaft by the smoke and the gas, he, in some unexplained way, became separated from the rest, and wandered off alone. The next day a rescuing party found him in the mine-stable, dead. He lay there beside the body of his mule. Deprived of the presence of human beings in the hours of that dreadful night, he had sought the company of the beast that had long been his companion in daily labor — and they died together.

But he had thought of those who were dear to him, for on a rough board near by he had written with chalk the name of his father and of his mother, and of a little cousin who had been named for him. He was only twelve years old when he died, but the title of hero was never more fairly earned than it was by him.

CHAPTER XVI.

MINERS AND THEIR WAGES.

A GOOD miner may be called a "skilled workman," and, as such, he is entitled to greater compensation for his labor than an ordinary workman. He expects it and gets it. There are two principal systems by which payments are made to miners. The first is according to the number of cubic yards of coal cut, and the second is according to the number of tons of coal mined and sent out. The first, which is prevalent in the regions of steep-pitching seams, is followed because the coal may remain in the chamber for an indefinite time after being cut. The second, which in the Wyoming region is almost universal, is somewhat more complicated. A chamber is taken by two miners, but the account on the books of the coal company is usually kept in the name of only one of them, who is held to be the responsible member of the firm. For instance, "Patrick Collins & Co." work a chamber in Law Shaft, and the firm is so designated. The first thing they do is to adopt some distinctive mark which may be chalked on the sides of their loaded cars to distinguish them from the loaded cars from other chambers. The letters of the alphabet are frequently used by miners, but, in default of these, some simple design that cannot readily be mistaken for any other is put into service. The triangle △ is a very common symbol with them, so is the long, horizontal line, crossed by short vertical ones, thus: —|—|———|—. The miners call this a candle. When a car has been loaded the symbol is chalked on the side of it, together with a number which tells how many cars have been sent from the chamber during the day. For instance, when a mine car appears at the surface marked "△ 5" it means that the car is from a certain chamber designated by that symbol, and that this is the fifth car which has been sent from that chamber during the day. On its way from the head of the breaker to the dumping cradle, the loaded car passes over the platform of the weighing scales and registers its weight on the scale beam. This weight is quickly read by the weigh-master, is transferred to his book, and goes to make up the daily report. In some districts a system in which tickets are used instead of chalk marks is in vogue, and in other districts duplicate checks are employed, but everywhere the general features remain the same.

In order to get a chamber from any of the large mining corporations, a miner must apply in person to the mining superintendent. He must come well recommended, or he must be known as a skillful, industrious, and temperate workman. The responsibility of driving a chamber properly is not a small one, and mining companies choose to take as little risk as possible in the selection of their men. Having accepted an applicant for a chamber, the company makes a contract with him, usually a verbal one, to pay him at a certain rate per ton or yard for the coal mined by him. The rate, though not wholly uniform, on account of the greater or less difficulty of cutting coal at the different collieries, is practically the same throughout an entire district.

A miner working at full time and in a good seam will send out enough coal each month to amount, at the contract price, to $150. But his expenses for laborers' wages, powder, oil, fuse, etc., will amount to $75 per month, leaving him a net income of $75 per month. The laborer is also paid according to the number of tons of coal sent out, and his wages will probably average $2 per day. It is not often in these days of thin seams that these rates of income are exceeded. And when the mines are in operation only a portion of the time, as is now often the case, these figures are seriously reduced.

The subject of wages frequently has been under discussion between miners and operators, and the differences of opinion on it have been prolific of many strikes. By some corporations and at some collieries a sliding scale has been adopted. That is, the miner has been paid, not at a fixed rate, but at a rate which constantly adjusts itself to the market price of coal. The objection to this method is said to be that the great companies who practically control the anthracite coal business form syndicates, fix the market price of their coal for a certain period of time, and then limit the output of each member of the syndicate to a certain number of tons during that period.

It is certain that no scheme of payment has yet been devised which is perfectly satisfactory to the great body of workers in the mines. But it is true also that employer and employee are working together more harmoniously now than they have worked at any time in the past, and that long and stubborn strikes of miners are growing, year by year, less frequent. It is to be hoped that the time will come when even the strike will not be considered necessary as a weapon of defense for the workman. As a rule strikes result in loss, and in loss only, to both capital and labor; and, as a rule also, labor suffers from them more than does capital, and this is the saddest feature of the case. Hon. Carroll D. Wright, the National Commissioner of Labor, has compiled the statistics of miners' strikes in Pennsylvania for the years 1881 to 1886 inclusive. His tables show that of 880 such strikes, which was the total number that occurred during the period named, 186 succeeded, 52 partly succeeded, and 642 failed. The loss to employers resulting from these strikes was $1,549,219; the loss to employees was $5,850,382; and the assistance given to the strikers during the periods of suspension amounted to $101,053. These figures form the best commentary to be had on the subject of strikes; they are eloquent with tales of hardship, of suffering, and of despair.

In those regions which have had long immunity from strikes, and in which work at full time has been the rule, the mine-workers are not only comfortable, but frequently are prosperous. They rarely occupy rooms in the cheap tenement houses of the towns, even if such occupancy would be to their convenience. They prefer to live in the outlying districts, where they can have homes of their own and gardens that they may cultivate. In the colliery villages the lots are usually laid out and sold or rented by the mining company to its workmen. Rent is not high, and, in case of sale, a long term contract is given, so that payments are in easy installments. The miner prefers to own his house and lot. Such ownership has a tendency to impress any man with the importance and responsibility of his duty as a citizen, and the miner is no exception to the rule. He is apt to waste neither his time nor his money when he has property and a family to care for. He tries, too, to lay by something for a rainy day; he knows that the probabilities are that either he or his family will eventually need it. As his hours of labor are

comparatively short he has considerable leisure
which he may spend profitably or foolishly as he
will. Many of the men spend this leisure working in their gardens or about their premises. It is
seldom that any of them go so far as to have regular extra employment to occupy their time while
out of the mines. Indeed the prevailing tendency
among miners is to do as little work as possible
outside of the mines. The opinion seems to be
prevalent among them that when a miner has cut
his coal he has done his full duty for the day, and
is entitled then to rest and recreation. He does
not take kindly to other kinds of work. He rarely
deserts his occupation of mining to take up any
other calling, and it may be said that after he has
passed middle age he never does. There is a fascination to the old miner about the dark chambers, the black walls, the tap of the drill, the
crash of falling coal, the smell of powder smoke
in the air, a fascination that is irresistible. He
would almost rather die in the familiar gloom of
the mine than live and toil in the sunlight on the
surface. Years of walking under the low mine
roofs have bent his back, have thrown his head
and shoulders forward, have given him that long
swinging stride characteristic of old miners. His
face is always pale; this is due, no doubt, to the
absence of sunlight in his working place; but,
as a rule, his general health is good; except when
he has worked for a long time in dry and dusty

mines. In that case he is apt to find himself, sooner or later, a victim to the disease known as "miner's consumption." The miner's appearance, as he passes along the street or road on his way home from his work, is, to eyes unaccustomed to the sight, anything but favorable. He wears heavy, hobnailed shoes or boots, flannel shirt, coarse jacket and pantaloons, all of them black with coal dirt and saturated with oil. He has a habit, when he comes from his work, of throwing his coat loosely about his shoulders, and wearing it so as he goes to his home. He usually wears a cap on his head, sometimes a slouch hat, rarely the helmet or fireman's hat with which artists are accustomed to picture him. This latter is too heavy and clumsy for common use; he only puts it on when working in places where water comes down freely on his head. Hooked to the front of his cap is the little tin lamp already described. When he goes to or comes from his work in the dark he allows it to burn and light him on his way. His face and hands are also black with coal dirt and powder smoke, and his features are hardly recognizable. The predominating race among the mine workers is the Irish, next in point of numbers comes the Welsh, then follow the Scotch and English, and, finally, the German. Of late years, however, Hungarian, Italian, and Russian laborers have come to the mines in large numbers, especially in the southern districts. These people can hardly be compared with the English or German speaking races; they do not become citizens of the country, have in the main no family life, and are, in a certain sense, slaves whose masters are their own countrymen.

In speaking of the characteristics of the mine workers as a class, it may be well, and it certainly is just, to correct a misapprehension concerning them which has become prevalent. From reading the descriptions given by newspaper correspondents and by certain writers of fiction, many people have come to think that all miners are little less than outlaws, that they are rude, ignorant, brutal in their instincts, and blind in their passions and animosities. This is very far indeed from the truth. Mine workers, as a class, are peaceful, law-abiding, intelligent citizens. That they are economical and industrious is well attested by the comfortable appearance of their homes, and the modest deposits that are made, in large numbers, in the numerous miner's savings banks of the different districts. There are, indeed, among them those who are intemperate, those who are coarse and violent, a disgrace to themselves and a menace to society. These are always the ones who come to the surface at a time when strained relations exist between employers and employees, and by their harsh language and unlawful conduct in the name of oppressed labor call down just retribution on themselves, but unjust condemnation on the true mine workers, who compose ninety-nine one hundredths of the class, but who do not go about drinking, ranting, destroying property, and inciting to crime. The proportion of "good-for-naughts" among the miners, however, is no greater than it is among any other class of workmen having the same numbers, and the same advantages and disadvantages. With the exception of the Hungarians, Russians, Italians, and Poles, of whom mention has already been made, the miners and their families compare favorably with any class of workers in the same grade of labor in America. Many of them indeed attain to prominent and responsible positions in business and society. Not a few of the clerks, merchants, contractors, mining engineers, bankers, lawyers, preachers, of the coal regions of to-day have stepped into those positions from the chambers of the mines, and have filled them admirably. The miner is fond of his family; his children are dear to him, and, whenever the grim necessities of life permit, he sends them to the schools instead of to the mines or breakers. He wishes to prepare them for a larger enjoyment of life than he himself has had, even though that life should be spent in the occupation which he himself has followed. And, indeed, there are few other occupations in which the possibilities of advancement are so great and so favorable. There must be mine bosses, mine inspectors, mine superintendents, and many of them, and they are, as a rule, promoted from the ranks. Young men of character, skill, and judgment are almost sure to step into the higher places.

If it were not for two evils that constantly menace and hamper him, the coal miner of to-day would be the most favored of workmen. These twin evils are strikes and lockouts. Abolish them and there would be no more comfortable, happy, and generally prosperous class of people in America than the workers in the coal mines.

GLOSSARY OF MINING TERMS.

After damp. The mixture of gases resulting from the burning of fire damp.

Air shaft. A vertical opening into a mine for the passage of air.

Airway. Any passage in the mine along which an air current passes; but the term is commonly applied to that passage which is driven, for ventilating purposes, parallel to and simultaneously with the gangway.

Anticlinal. A fold of strata in which the inclination of the sides of the fold is from the axis downward.

Barrier pillars. Large pillars of coal left at a boundary line, or on the outskirts of a squeeze.

Basin. The hollow formed by a fold of the seam; any large area of included coal.

Battery. In steep-pitching seams, a wooden structure built across the shute to hold the mined coal back.

Bearing in. Cutting a horizontal groove at the bottom or side of the face of a breast.

Bed. Any separate stratum of rock or coal.

Bench. A horizontal section of the coal seam, included between partings of slate or shale.

Black damp. Carbonic acid gas; known also as choke damp.

Blossom. Decomposed coal, indicating the presence of an outcrop.

Blower. A forcible and copious discharge of gas from a cavity in the coal seam.

Bony coal. Coal containing in its composition slaty or argillaceous material.

Bore-hole. A hole of small diameter drilled or bored, either vertically or horizontally, through the measures or in the coal; usually, a hole drilled vertically for prospecting purposes.

Brattice. A partition made of boards or of brattice cloth, and put up to force the air current to the face of the workings.

Breaker. A building, with its appliances, used in the preparation of anthracite coal for the market.

Break-through. A cross-heading or entrance, used in the bituminous mines.

Breast. The principal excavation in the mine from which coal is taken; known also as chamber.

Broken coal. One of the regular sizes of prepared anthracite.

Buckwheat coal. One of the regular sizes of prepared anthracite.

Buggy. A small car or wagon used for transporting coal from the working face to the gangway.

Buntons. The timbers placed crosswise of a shaft down its entire depth, dividing it into vertical compartments.

Butt. In bituminous coal seams, the vertical planes of cleavage at right angles to the face cleavage.

Butty. A comrade; a fellow-worker in the same chamber.

Cage. See Carriage.

Carriage. The apparatus on which coal is hoisted in a shaft.

Cartridge pin. A round stick of wood on which the paper tube for the cartridge is formed.

Cave-hole. A depression at the surface, caused by a fall of roof in the mine.

Chain pillars. Heavy pillars of coal, lining one or both

GLOSSARY OF MINING TERMS. 235

sides of the gangway, and left for the protection of that passage.

Chamber. See Breast.

Chestnut coal. One of the regular sizes of prepared anthracite.

Choke damp. See After-damp.

Cleavage. The property of splitting on a certain plane.

Collar. The upper horizontal crosspiece uniting the legs in the timbering of a drift, tunnel, slope, or gangway.

Colliery. All the workings of one mine, both underground and at the surface.

Conglomerate. The rock strata lying next beneath the coal measures.

Counter-gangway. A gangway which is tributary to the main gangway, and from which a new section of coal is worked.

Cracker boss. The officer in charge of the screen room in a breaker.

Creep. A crush in which the pillars are forced down into the floor or up into the roof of the mine.

Cribbing. The timber lining of a shaft, extending usually from the surface to bed-rock.

Crop-fall. A caving in of the surface at the outcrop.

Cross-heading. A narrow opening for ventilation, driven through a wall of coal separating two passages or breasts.

Crush. A settling downward of the strata overlying a portion of an excavated coal seam.

Culm. All coal refuse finer than buckwheat size.

Dip. The angle which any inclined stratum makes with a horizontal line.

Door boy. A boy who opens and shuts the door placed across any passageway in the mines to control the direction of the ventilating current.

Double entry. One of the systems by which openings into the bituminous coal mines are made.

GLOSSARY OF MINING TERMS.

Downcast. The passage or way through which air is drawn into a mine.

Drift. A water-level entrance to a mine, driven in from the surface on the coal.

Drill. Any tool used for boring holes in the rock or coal.

Driving. Excavating any horizontal passage in or into the mines.

Drum. A revolving cylinder, at the head of any hoisting-way, on which the winding rope is coiled.

Egg coal. One of the regular sizes of prepared anthracite.

—Entrance. See Cross-heading.

Entry. The main entrance and traveling road in bituminous mines.

Face. The end wall at the inner or working extremity of any excavation in or into the mines. In bituminous mines the vertical plane of cleavage at right angles to the butt cleavage.

Fan. A machine used to force a ventilating current of air through a mine.

Fault. A displacement of strata in which the measures on one side of a fissure are pushed up above the corresponding measures on the other side.

Fire-board. A blackboard, fixed near the main entrance of a mine, on which the fire boss indicates each morning the amount and location of dangerous gases.

Fire boss. An official whose duty it is to examine the workings for accumulations of dangerous gases.

Fire clay. The geological formation which is usually found immediately underlying a coal bed.

Fire damp. Light carbureted hydrogen.

Fissure. A separation of rock or coal across the measures.

Floor. The upper surface of the stratum immediately underlying a coal seam.

Gangway. An excavation or passageway, driven in the coal, at a slight grade, forming the base from which the other workings of the mine are begun.

Gas. Fire damp.

Gob. The refuse separated from the coal and left in the mine.

Guides. Narrow vertical strips of timber at each side of the carriage way in shafts, to steady and guide the carriage in its upward or downward movement.

Gunboat. A car used for hoisting coal on steep slopes.

Head-frame. The frame erected at the head of a shaft to support the sheaves and hold the carriage.

Heading. Synonymous with gangway. Any separate continous passage used as a traveling way or as an airway.

Hopper. A feeding shute or pocket in a breaker.

Horseback. A small ridge in the roof or floor of a coal seam.

Inside slope. An inclined plane in a mine, on which coal is hoisted from a lower to a higher level.

Jacket. One of the sections or frames of wire mesh of which a revolving screen is made up.

Keeps. Projections of wood or iron on which the carriage rests while it is in place at the head of the shaft.

Lagging. Small timbers or planks driven in behind the legs and over the collars to give additional support to the sides and roof of the passage.

Legs. The inclined sticks on which the collar rests in gangway, tunnel, drift, and slope timbering.

Lift. All the workings driven from one level in a steep-pitching seam.

Loading place. The lowest extremity of the breaker, where prepared coal is loaded into railway cars.

Lump coal. The largest size of prepared anthracite.

Manway. A passageway in or into the mine, used as a footway for workmen.

Mouth. The opening, at the surface, of any way into the mines.

Needle. An instrument used in blasting coal, with which a channel is formed through the tamping for the entrance of the squib.

Nut coal. One of the regular sizes of bituminous coal.

Opening. Any excavation in or into a mine.

Operator. The person, firm, or corporation working a colliery.

Outcrop. That portion of any geological stratum which appears at the surface.

Output. The amount of coal produced from any mine, or from any area of country.

Parting. The layer of slate or bony coal which separates two benches of a coal seam.

Pea coal. One of the regular sizes of prepared anthracite.

Picking shute. A shute in the breaker from which the pieces of slate are picked out by a boy as they pass down with the coal.

Pillar. A column or body of coal left unmined to support the roof.

Pillar and breast. The name of a common mining method.

Pinch. See Crush.

Pitch. See Dip.

Plane. Any incline on which a track is laid for the purpose of lowering or hoisting coal.

Pockets. Receptacles at the lower ends of shutes, in breakers, from which coal is loaded into railway cars.

GLOSSARY OF MINING TERMS. 239

Post. A wooden prop to support the roof in bituminous mines.

Prop. A timber set at right angles to the seam, in anthracite mines, to support the roof.

Prospecting. Searching for indications of coal on the surface, and testing coal seams from the surface.

Pump way. That compartment of a shaft or slope down which the pump rods and pipes are extended.

Rib. The side of an excavation as distinguished from the end or face.

Rob. To mine coal from the pillars after the breasts are worked out.

Rock tunnel. A tunnel driven through rock strata.

Rolls. In breakers, heavy iron or steel cylinders set with teeth, used for breaking coal.

Roof. The stratum immediately overlying a coal seam. The rock or coal overhead in any excavation.

Room. Synonymous with breast or chamber; used in bituminous mines.

Safety lamp. A lamp that can be carried into inflammable gases without igniting them.

Scraper. A tool used for cleaning out bore holes in blasting.

Screen. Any apparatus used for separating coal into different sizes; usually, the revolving cylinder of wire mesh in a breaker.

Seam. A stratum of coal.

Separator. A machine for picking slate.

Shaft. A vertical entrance into a mine.

Sheave. The wheel in the head-frame that supports the winding rope.

Shift. The time during which a miner or laborer works continuously, alternating with some other similar period.

Shute. A narrow passageway through which coal descends

by gravity from the foot of the breast to the gangway; an inclined trough, in a breaker, down which coal slides by gravity.

Single entry. One of the systems by which bituminous mines are entered.

Slack. The dirt from bituminous coal.

Slate picker. A boy who picks slate from coal. A machine used for the same purpose.

Slope. An entrance to a mine driven down through an inclined coal seam. Inside slope: a passage in the mine driven down through the seam, by which to bring coal up from a lower level.

Slope carriage. A platform on wheels on which cars are raised and lowered in steep slopes.

Smut. See Blossom.

Split. A branch of a ventilating air current.

Spread. The bottom width of a slope, drift, tunnel, or gangway between the legs of the timbering.

Squeeze. See Crush.

Squib. A powder cracker used for igniting the cartridge in blasting.

Steamboat coal. One of the regular sizes of prepared anthracite.

Stopping. A wall built across an entrance or any passage to control the ventilating current.

Stove coal. One of the regular sizes of prepared anthracite.

Strike. The direction of a line drawn horizontally along any stratum.

Stripping. Mining coal by first removing the surface down to the coal bed ; open working.

Sump. A basin in mines entered by a slope or shaft, in which the water of the mine is collected to be pumped out.

Swamp. A depression in the seam.

Synclinal. A fold of strata in which the inclination of the sides is from the axis upward.

Tipple. In the bituminous regions, a building in which coal is dumped, screened, and loaded into boats or cars.
Trapper. See Door boy.
Traveling way. A passageway for men and mules in or into the mines.
Trip. The number of cars less than enough to constitute a train drawn at one time by any motive power.
Tunnel. An opening into a mine driven horizontally across the measures.

Under-clay. See Fire clay.
Underholing. See Bearing in.
Upcast. An opening from a mine through which air is taken out.

Vein. Used (improperly) synonymously with seam, bed, or stratum.

Wagon. A mine car.
Waste. Gob; coal dirt.
Water level. An entrance into or passage in a mine, driven with just sufficient grade to carry off water.
White damp. Carbonic oxide.
Wings. See Keeps.
Work. To mine.
Working face. A face at which mining is being done.
Workings. The excavations of a mine, taken as a whole; or, more particularly, that portion of the mine in which mining is being done.

INDEX.

Accidents resulting from falls, 126; to boys, 218.
Act of 1885, 88.
After damp, composition of, etc., 167.
Air currents in mines, 148, 149.
Air, deterioration of, in mines, 147, 152.
Airways, beginning of, 95.
Allen, Nicholas, 49, 62.
Ancients, use of coal by, 35.
Animal life of Carboniferous era, 18.
Anthracite coal, analysis of, 6; commercial sizes of, 181; description of, 8; ignition of, 59; of bituminous origin, 25; skill in mining, 192.
Anticlinals, 25.
Appalachian Range, 3.
Archean time, 3.
Areas of coal measures, 31; of Pennsylvania coal fields, 33, 34.
Avondale Mine, disaster at, 173.

Baltimore vein, 75.
Basin in a coal seam, 29.
Battery in steep chambers, 108.
Bearing in, in bituminous mines, 197.
Benches in coal seams, 23-115.
Bituminous coal, analysis of, 7; description of 8; process of mining, 194.
Black damp, composition, etc., 169.
Blasting in mines, 119, 120, 125, 131.
Blossom of coal, 77.
Blower of gas, 160.
Boys, accidents to, 218; amusements of, 219; at tipple work, 202; characteristics of, 217; duties of, at breaker, 215; in British coal mines, 205.
Boy door-tenders, duties of, 214.
Boy drivers, duties of, 210.
Braddock's road, 40.
Brattice at face of chamber, 103.
Breaker, description of, 179; location of, 178; 183; passage of coal through, 185; picking shutes in, 186; structure and appearance of, 184.
Break through, in bituminous mines, 195.
Breast. See Chamber.
Bryden, Alexander, 143.
Bryden, Andrew, 140, 168.
Buildings at mouth of shaft, 176.
Buntons in shaft, 89.
Butler, Col. Lord, 56.
Butt cleavage in bituminous mines, 194.
Butty, 114.

Calamities, 17.
Candles, use of, in mines, 162.
Cannel coal, 6, 13.
Carbondale Mines, fall in, 140.
Carboniferous age, 3.
Carboniferous era, animal life of, 18.
Carboniferous plants, 14-16.
Carriage in shaft, 90.
Cartridge, how made and used, 117.
Cave holes, 137.
Cenozoic time, 4.
Chain pillars, 109.
Chamber, car track in, 103; description of, 100; length of, 102; scene at face of, 131.
Charcoal, process of formation, 10.
Charles, John, 50.
Chest, miner's, 120.
Choke damp, 169.
Cist, Charles, 48.
Cist, Jacob, 52, 58.
Coal, classification of, 7; originally all bituminous, 12; origin of, 8; production, by corporations, 70; specific gravity of, what is it? 6.
Coal dust, explosive quality of, 172.
Coal lands, division of, 69; investments in, 68; leasing of, 71; value of, 70.
Coal mining by corporations, 72.
Coal plants, age of, 3.
Coal seams, number and thickness of, 22, 23.

INDEX.

Coal-waste, heaps of, 191.
Conglomerate, 76.
Conifers, 17.
Corve, in British coal mines, 205.
Cost of different methods of entry, 92.
Counter-gangway, 105.
Crahan, Martin, story of, 220.
Creeping pillars, 136.
Crezot Mine, accident at, 170.
Crop falls, 139.
Cross-headings, 95.
Crowbar, miner's tool, 121.
Crust of earth, subsidence of, etc., 24.
" Cry of the Children," Mrs. Browning's, 207.
Culm, its disposition and use, 190.
Curr, John, 90.

Davy, Sir Humphrey, experiments of, 162.
Decapitation of coal seams, 29.
Delaware and Hudson gravity railroad, 66; canal, 66.
Diamond drill, 79.
Dip of strata, 29.
Door boy, duties of, etc., 149, 214.
Doors in mines, 149.
Drainage in mines, 154.
Drift, as a mode of entry, 80.
Drilling, by diamond drill, 79; by hand, 78; by rope method, 78; by spring pole method, 78.
Drill, machine hand, 116; miner's, 116.
Driver boss, his duties, etc., 113.
Driver boy, duties of, etc., 113, 210, 213.
Dump shute bars in breaker, 185.

Eagle Shaft, disaster at, 168.
Early mining methods, 94.
Eastern middle coal field, 33.
Electricity in breakers, 217; in mines, 105, 122, 127, 213.
Enaliosaurs, 20.
Entrances in mines, 101.
Entries in bituminous mines, 195, 196.
Evans, Oliver, 52.
Experiments with anthracite, 52, 53.

Face cleavage in bituminous mines, 194.
Face of chamber, 101.
Falls of roof and coal, 125, 135.
Fan for ventilation, 151.
Fault in strata, 26.
Felling Colliery, disaster at, 162.
Fell, Judge Jesse, 53.

Females in British coal mines, 206.
Ferns of coal era, 16.
Fire boss, duties of, etc., 112, 166.
Fire damp, characteristics of, 160; explosions of, 161; in abandoned workings, 166.
Fishes, age of, 3; of Carboniferous age, 19.
Fissures in strata, 26.
Flanigan, John, 94.
Flowers in Carboniferous age, 21.

Gangways, beginning of, 95; description of, 97; direction of, 98; driving, 113; length of, 104; walking in, 129.
Gases not confined to coal measures, 159.
Germany, mining of coal in, 37.
Ginther, Philip, 47.
Girls in British coal mines, 205.
Gore, Obadiah, experiments of, 45.
Graff, Frederick, 52.
Great Summit Mine, 57.
Guibal, inventor of fan, 152.
Guides in shaft, 90.

Hammer, miner's, 121.
Head-frame at mouth of shaft, 177.
Health of mine workers, 153.
Hennepin, Father, explorer, 38.
Hillegas, Michael, 48.
Hoisting apparatus at shaft, 177.
Hollenback, Colonel George M., 56.
Horsebacks in coal seams, 28.
Hosie, John, adventure of, 145.
Hurrier in British mines, 205.

Inclined planes in mines, 105.
Indians, coal known to, 37, 43, 44.
Inside slopes, 106.
Invertebrates, age of, 3.
Investments in coal lands, 68.

Jenkins, Henry, 180.

Laborers, duties of, etc., 114, 122.
Lackawanna region, early coal trade in, 65.
Lagging, its use, etc., 82.
Lamp, miner's, 121.
Laplace, astronomer, 1.
Lehigh coal, early trade in, 57, 58, 62.
Lepidodendrids, 17.
Lesehot, inventor, 79.
Lift mining, 85, 107.
Light carbureted hydrogen, 159.
Lignite, 6, 11.
Loading place in breaker, 189.

INDEX.

Localities in which coal is found, 31, 32.
Locomotives in mines, 199.
London, burning of coal in, 36.
Long wall mining system, 110.
Loyalsock coal field, 34.
Lump coal, bituminous, 202.

Machine for mining soft coal, 197.
Mammals, age of, 4, 12.
Man, age of, 4.
Marsh gas, composition of, etc., 160.
Mellen and Bishop, experimenters, 64.
Mesozoic time, 4.
Mine, anthracite, number of employees in, 112.
Mine boss, duties, etc., 112.
Mine car, 123.
Mine, darkness in a, 133; in an abandoned, 134; silence in a deserted, 132.
Mine law of 1870 and 1885, 208.
Miner, Charles, 58.
Miner, appearance of, 227; character and ambition of, 230; clothing of, 228; duties of, etc., 114, 122, 124; home and outside occupation of, 226; nativity of, 228.
Mines, flooding of, 156.
Miocene period, 12.
Mules in mines, 212.

Nanticoke, accident at, 157.
Nebular Hypothesis, 1.
Needle, miner's, 117.
Newcastle, carrying coals to, 37.
Nobles, David, hunter, 65.
Northern coal field, 33.
Nut coal, bituminous, 202.

Open quarry mining, 80.
Outcrop of strata, 29, 75.

Paleozoic time, 3.
Pannier women in British mines, 205.
Paris, burning of coal in, 37.
Partings in coal seams, 23.
Peat, 6, 11.
Pennsylvania, coal fields of, 32, 33, 34.
Picking machine in breaker, 187.
Picking shute in breaker, 186.
Pick, miner's, 121.
Pillar and breast mining system, 99.
Pillars at foot of shaft, 95; creeping, 136; robbing of, 133; slipping, 136.
Pinch in a coal mine, 28.
Pittsburgh, coal beds near, 193; coal trade of, 42; discovery of coal near, 41.
Pittsburg, Kansas, disaster at, 172.
Pockets in breaker, 189.
Props, use and setting of, 114.
Prospecting for coal, 75.
Pump mining, 155.
Pumpway in shaft, 155.
Putter, in British mines, 205.

Rats in mines, 212.
Reptiles, age of, 4, 12.
Rhode Island, coal in, 32, 40.
Rib of coal, 101.
Richmond coal field, 38.
Robbing pillars, 133.
Robinson, John W., 58.
Rocky Mountains, 20.
Rolls in breaker, 179.
Rolls in coal seams, 28.
Rooms in bituminous mines, 195.
Run of mine, bituminous coal, 202.

Safety carriage, 91.
Safety lamps, how to use, 165; invention of, 163.
Schuylkill region, early coal trade in, 62, 64.
Scotland, mining of coal in, 37.
Scraper, in bituminous mines, 198.
Scraper, use of, 117.
Screen, revolving, in breaker, 180.
Semi-anthracite coal, 8.
Shaft, compartments of, 89; descending a, 128; foot of, 128; in bituminous mines, 199; in steep-pitching seams, 109; location and depth of, 86; sinking of, 87; water in, while sinking, 154.
Sheaves in head-frame, 177.
Shoemaker, Colonel George, 62.
Shovel, miner's, 121.
Sigillariæ, 17.
Slack, bituminous waste, 202.
Slate picker's duties, etc., 186.
Sledge, miner's, 121.
Slipping pillars, 136.
Slope, dimensions of, 85; entrance by, 84; in steep-pitching seams, 85.
Smith, Abijah, 56.
Smith, John, 56.
Smut of coal, 77.
Southern coal field, 32.
Sphagnum, 11.
Splits of the air current, 148.
Squeeze in a mine, 28, 136.
Squib, use of, 118.
Stair shaft in bituminous mines, 200.
States in which coal is found, 31, 32.
Steep-pitching seams, mining in, 107.

Stigmaria, 18.
Stockton Mines, accident at, 139.
Strike of strata, 29.
Strikes among miners, 225.
Summit Hill Mine, 80.
Sump in mine, 96.
Surface, disturbance of, by falls, 138.
Susquehanna River, coal trade, 41.
Swamp in mines, 29.
Symbols marked on cars, 223.
Synclinals, 25.

Tamping, process of, 118.
Temperature in mines, 210.
Terrace in coal outcrop, 77.
Theophrastus, 35.
Tipple, at the bituminous mines, 201, 203.
Tunnel, entrance by, 82.
Tunnels in mine interiors, 84, 106.
Turnbull, William, 58.

Ventilation by fan, 151; by open furnace, 150; in bituminous mines, 199; principle of, in mines, 97, 148.
Von Storch, H. C. L., 65.

Wages of miners, 224; computing and payment of, 222; of boys, 213-215; sliding scale for computing, 224.
Waste in coal mining, 134; of the coal measures, 28.
Water, driving workings toward, 155; in mine, 96; tonnage of, hoisted, 155.
Weighing coal, 223.
Weiss, Colonel Jacob, 48.
Western middle coal field, 33.
West Pittston, disaster at, 175.
White & Hazard, coal trade of, 62; experiments of, 60.
Wilcox, Crandal, 56.
Wings in shaft, 91.
Woodward breaker, 121.
Working pillars, 136.
Wright, Joseph, 56.
Wurts, William and Maurice, 65.
Wyoming coal field, 33.
Wyoming valley, discovery of coal in, 45; early coal trade of, 56.

Ziegler, Charles W., 188.

www.ingramcontent.com/pod-product-compliance
Lightning Source LLC
Chambersburg PA
CBHW032109230426
43672CB00009B/1678